# Climber's Guide to
# Sedona and Oak Creek Canyon
## A Better Way to Die

Tim Toula

## Chockstone Press, Inc.
Evergreen, CO. 80439

CLIMBER'S GUIDE TO SEDONA AND OAK CREEK CANYON: A BETTER WAY TO DIE

Cover Photos: View east from Chimney Rock. Photo by Tim Toula.
     (inset): Andy Marquardt jumping accross to the lower summit of the Mace. Photo by Bill Hatcher.

ISBN: 0-934641-16-1

PUBLISHED AND DISTRIBUTED BY:
Chockstone Press, Inc.
PO Box 3505
Evergreen, Colorado 80439

# DEDICATION

To my Pop and all the other Bohemians of the world:

May St. Wenceslaus watch over you.

And also to the destitute and homeless. Rev. William Sloane Coffin pastor at NYC's Riverside Church and Head of SANE/FREEZE Campaign for Global security says "Already we've gone too far when, on any given night, 100,000 American children go to sleep homeless. And we house our missiles so much better than we do our homeless."

Please feel free to send any new route information, corrections, questions, comments, and/or obscenities to the author in care of the publisher. All will be appreciated, especially chicken-scratched, blood-stained topos.

# THANKS

My sincere thanks to all who have helped with this guide: George Bain, Alan Bartlett, Steve Bartlett, Scott Baxter, Jon Bernhard, Rand Black, Dave Bloom, Jeff Bowman, Tim Coats, Larry Coats, Richard Cilley, Dow Davis, Chris Dunn, Mike Hill, Mike Hren, Dave Houchin, Allen Humphrey, Dave Insley, John Middendorf, Stan Mish, Geoff Parker, Courtney Phillips, Ron Plapp (USFS), Glen Rink, Reed Thorne, Walt Shipley, Darren Singer, Jim Symans, Ray Yought, Kathy Zaiser, and any others whom I may have inadvertently missed.

# PREFACE

*You may tie your shoestrings in the morning, but the undertaker may untie them before night.*

*Are you ready to meet your maker?*

You've learned how to fly, now check out how to die. *A Better Way to Die* was a slow and painful effort on my part to taunt climbers with some of the scariest and hairiest rock climbing abounding in the scenic vicinity of Sedona and Oak Creek Canyon, Arizona. After *A Cheap Way to Fly: Free Climbing Guide to Northern Arizona*, (y'know, the guide with all those artistic drawings and incredibly clear maps and topos?… How 'bout the ones your cursed me for? Yeah, OK, now you remember) I never dreamed I'd be fingering another lead stick again. But, like thousands of other climbaholics, I'm broke and trying to get out of debt fast? So why not pop other poor and bewildered climbers for a few pfennings worth of new area information. I've promised to add photos, improve graphics, accuracy, and help you, the unknowing climber, come to grips with that lurks in these canyonlands, so help me Sedona Schnebly. (Also thrown in is a smattering of wit. At no extra charge.)

This is a collection of available information. It is by no means final. While I have snooped around and done a fair share of the climbs here, I claim no absolute authority about this landmaze. That is, Sedona and the back of my hand do *not* look alike.

Every new guidebook seems to make the world a little smaller. But anyone who studies the maps and topos presented here, can see how many new worlds await. Every day reveals another secret. This guide, then, is a beginning. A starter for self-discovery. Remember, it's not just a guide, it's an adventure! It should enable one, at worst, to retrace old routes and, at best, to feel new breezes on virgin sandstone. Or, it may provide the chance to meet your Maker?

*Only those are fit to live who do not fear to die.*
Teddy Roosevelt

# TABLE OF CONTENTS

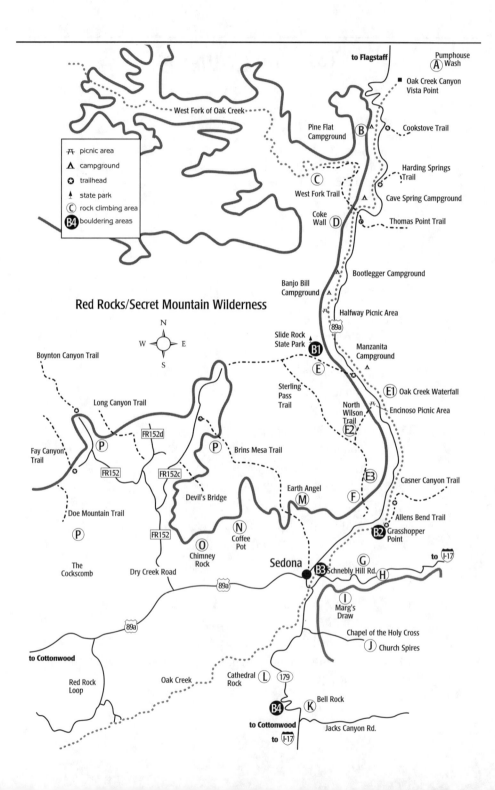

# INTRODUCTION

What's worse than being a stowaway with a kamikaze? Allow me to introduce you to the quintessential nightmare of your climbing dreams—the sandstone climbs of Oak Creek Canyon and Sedona, Arizona. That's right, Sedona, Arizona is the funereal home of some of the scariest climbing in the USA. I've always thought, "Wouldn't it be great if all the rock in Sedona were granite!" What a climber's mecca! What a sweet dream! But as Tennessee Williams wrote in *Suddenly Last Summer*, nature is not made in the image of man's compassion. Despite the amount of rock present, much of it in many climbers' eyes is as worthless as a Mexican peso. Rightly so, for the rock can be sandy, friable, hollow, unprotectable, choked with loose blocks, and let's see…oh yeah, and otherwise pure shi … junk. The good Lord should've banned it from the earth. But perhaps he wanted to show climbers how a landscape so intricately beautiful could be so deceptively deadly. Not that the rock is the only threat in this barbarian terrain. The plants, too, can be as vicious as she-lions that have clawed down bullocks.

But if you're a thrillseeker, one who loves living on the edge, you may have found your niche. I'm not talking about cheap thrills like drinking milk after its expiration date or going for a swim after an Ahwahnee Sunday Brunch. No, this is the place for those who would welcome the sweet delight of danger, venture to the edge of doom and stare death in the eye to hear its footsteps saunter off. But beware, lest you sleep the sleep from which men never recover, the fingers of death touch many.

On any given day, I've witnessed edges snap, hand jams explode, bolt studs wiggle and bolthangers revolve in the wind. I've seen whole pitches without one dependable hold. I've heard tell of climbers taking massive falls only to live. And yes, I've even awoke in a cold sweat to see myself strung out on yet another horrorshow climb. It's never pretty.

Still, if you think mantling on dirt hummocks, traversing unprotected for 40 feet, or clipping into your first bolt while standing on a stack of saltine crackers 20 feet up is better than paying $5 to watch Nightmare on Elm Street, then read on! You meet the stringent requirements of insanity all aspiring Sedona climbers must have to proliferate in red rock climbing. If, however, all this doesn't sound like your brand of fun, STOP reading this guidebook now and go catch the movies. Your chance of enjoying red rock climbing is slimmer than winning on the baccarat tables in Vegas. Still, should the comforts of modern daily living begin to dull your senses, let Sedona provide the proper therapy by putting you back in touch with one of your first Neanderthal instincts: Survival!

Please don't let this intro scare you off from enjoying all the great climbing that exists in the Sedona Area. For after all, anyone who has experienced more than just the Mace knows that the climbing here is never scarewee, just healthy…fun…ha…haha…fun…hahaha…hahahahaha…

*For those of you who consider life to be a joke, consider the punchline.*

## HOW TO USE THIS GUIDE

Most people just read it, but should an emergency arise *A Better Way to Die* provides 6400 BTUs of heat lasting approximately 25 minutes if benighted on a spire. Also, it's handy for unexpected toilet paper drought. (Leave route list and topos for last.)

In writing this guide, it is my intention to give the out-of-town climber a comfortable feel for the Sedona/Oak Creek Canyon area. While the climbing is fascinating, the other facets of Sedona are equally so. Reading about the geology, biology, and human aspect of this canyonland environment can only enhance your trip. Information on local amenities and services is also included.

And now an explanation to the most important information within this guide: the climbing. Amid the other climbing hullabaloo, please find these important subjects: a General Climbing Area Map, the Sedona/OCC Climbing Route List with locator maps, Climber's Road Log, Selected Climbing Topos, and photos of formations.

First, study the General Climbing Area Map opposite page 1. From this, you will instantly know the location of the 16 "main areas" (denoted by capital letters A through P). Second, refer to the Route List. The List shows you exactly the routes in each area, their description, and an aerial sketch of each "main area" for easy, on-the-ground route locating. Third, the Climber's Road Log takes away the guesswork of figuring out where to park and distances between points plus other tidbits of info. Finally, phfeww, for those who want all the info they can get, Climbing Topos of Selected Routes. While finding most routes will be easy enough from the aerial views, the topos may clarify routefinding on some of the better climbs.

But that's not all you get when you buy this edition! THAT'S RIGHT! *A Better Way to Die* comes with photos for instant identification of many of Sedona's formations.

DOES IT COME WITH RADAR TOO?

A few other explanatory notes: In this guide be aware of frequent abbreviations, especially regarding directions. In such cases, the word is given followed by the abbreviation as in Oak Creek Canyon(OCC). Other standard examples are N for north, R for right, and so forth.

## GENERAL AREA INFO

Welcome then to Sedona, Arizona: a land of mild climate, rich retirees, Hollywood sets, creative artists, posh resorts, New Age thinkers, scenic sanctuaries, and yes, red death rock climbers. Sedona started as a tiny western settlement 94 years ago. Today, it is a recreation, business and retirement community of nearly 15,000 (and growing) healthy residents; a town set in what could be a national park; a sandstone San Diego. It offers climbers most of the modern amenities as does the Cottonwood area 20 miles west and Flagstaff 30 miles to the north. More on this later…

Where the human element leaves off, the climbing begins. And what a setting it is! With beckoning heights, Sedona invites. For what passing climber has not caressed the red rocks with their glance? Should your sense of adventure lead you to higher inclinations, so much the better. For this is a place to enjoy the earth as much as the triumphs of climbing; a place where the adventuresome climber can still expect to get away from it all.

This guide covers an approximate area of 25 square miles in this order: from Oak Creek Canyon (OCC) Overlook, 13 miles south of Flagstaff, down through Sedona to Jacks Canyon/Munds Mountain Wilderness and the Village of Oak Creek. It then turns back northwest to West Sedona and the Red Rock/Secret Mountain Wilderness Area ending up at Loy Butte. That's a lotta rocky real estate.

The sixteen-mile long Oak Creek Canyon, about a mile across and 2500' deep at its greatest dimensions, hosts an array of climbing features. At the OCC Overlook, basalt cliffs are first to entice the climber. This basalt area and others along the rim, like the Oak Creek Waterfall and Schnebly Hill, offer excellent hard rock cragging (for the weak of heart) and are covered in detail in *A Cheap Way to Fly: Free Climbing Guide to Northern Arizona. A Better Way to Die* covers mainly the soft rock sandstone cliffs and spires of OCC and Sedona, with the fantastic basalt cliffs of the Oak Creek Waterfall included. Below the Oak Creek Overlook lies Pumphouse Wash, a sandstone canyon where the routes in this guide begin.

After the Pumphouse Wash Bridge (at the base of the switchbacks), all of the sandstone routes lie to the west of Highway 89A (except Oak Creek Waterfall) until Grasshopper Point and eventually the north side of Schnebly Hill Road. The amazing West Fork is a large "side canyon" of Oak Creek, and a natural attraction in and of itself (also the site of novelist Zane Grey's *Call of the Canyon*). Take heed, the majority of the routes in OCC are sandy and scary, but do have short approaches usually less than 45 minutes. This popular recreational area gets heavy traffic use, so beware of death by Metallica.

Once in Sedona, a climber realizes the expanse of this sandstone arena. Routes range from a wealth of one-pitch pinnacles to multipitched backcountry walls. Perhaps the best way to acquaint a climber to their environs is via a trip to the Airport Mesa Vortex and the hill to the north. See drawing and photos on the next page. From the vantage point of Point 4874', one can behold the red rock buttes and pinnacles, and white Coconino sandstone cliffs that wrap around in a 270 degree fashion from west to north to southeast. Mingus Mountain can be seen to the southeast. A half-hour trip to Airport Road is worth more than I could possibly spout off here. So check it out!…and feel the power of the vortex upon you!

## Introduction
### Overview of Sedona Rock Climbing Formations

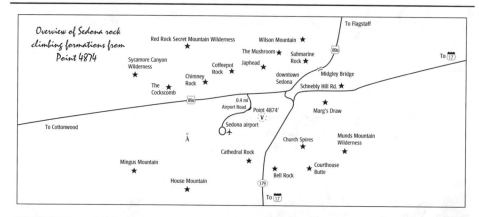

Overview of Sedona rock
climbing formations from
Point 4874

Red Rock Secret Mountain Wilderness ★

Wilson Mountain ★

To Flagstaff

Sycamore Canyon
Wilderness
★

The Mushroom ★    Submarine
Rock ★

89a

To 17

Coffeepot
Rock ★

Japhead ★

Chimney
Rock ★

downtown
Sedona

Midgley Bridge

The
Cockscomb ★

89a

Schnebly Hill Rd. ★

0.4 mi
Airport Road

Point 4874'
V

Marg's Draw ★

To Cottonwood

N
Å

Sedona airport ✈

Church Spires ★

Munds Mountain
Wilderness ★

Mingus Mountain
★

Cathedral Rock ★

House Mountain ★

Bell Rock ★

Courthouse
Butte ★

179

To 17

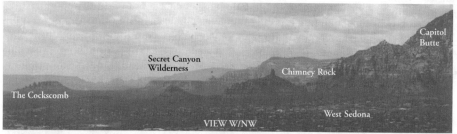

The Cockscomb

Secret Canyon
Wilderness

Chimney Rock

Capitol
Butte

West Sedona

VIEW W/NW

Chimney
Rock

Capitol
Butte

Coffee Pot
Rock

VIEW NW

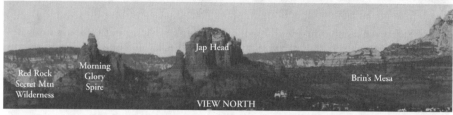

Red Rock
Secret Mtn
Wilderness

Morning
Glory
Spire

Jap Head

Brin's Mesa

VIEW NORTH

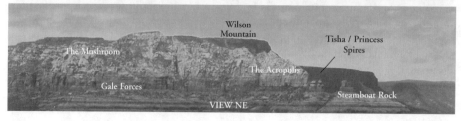

The Mushroom

Wilson
Mountain

Tisha / Princess
Spires

The Acropolis

Gale Forces

Steamboat Rock

VIEW NE

## Introduction
## Overview of Sedona Rock Climbing Formations

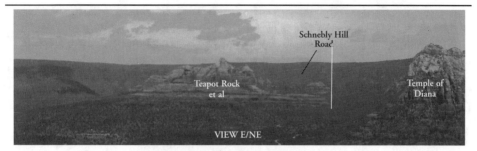

Schnebly Hill Road

Teapot Rock
et al

Temple of
Diana

VIEW E/NE

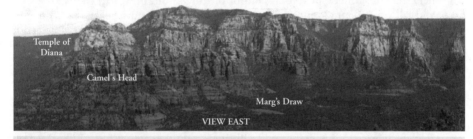

Temple of
Diana

Camel's Head

Marg's Draw

VIEW EAST

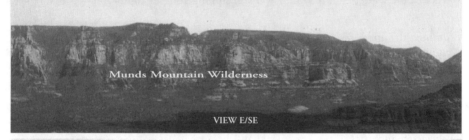

Munds Mountain Wilderness

VIEW E/SE

Twin Buttes

Courthouse Butte

Bell Rock

Point 5,246

VIEW SE

Cathedral
Rock

VIEW SOUTH

## WEATHER: (To be announced. Har, har...)

Great climbing may be had in Sedona/OCC during any given month of the year. This hinges on three variables: the given day, elevation, and solar aspect. Since there's not much you can do from day to day except check the forecast and put in your request with the Great Weathermaker. This leaves elevation and solar aspect.

Elevations in this guide range from 7196' at East Pocket Lookout to 4000' at Oak Creek Village. Such a broad gap makes for a highly variable "climbate" at any time of the year (as well as diverse flora and fauna). Solar heating also plays a big role in climbing comfort. As a general rule in summer, pick routes out of the direct sun. In winter, cherish the sun. Spring and fall you'll figure it out when you get there. This of course all depends on whether an individual is a lizard or a polar bear. The climbing area overview maps, besides showing route location, can assist you with route selection by showing their respective solar aspect.

Generally, as the season enters late April on through September, you'll want to start your approaches very early in the day (twilight?) to arrive at your climb fresh, i.e. hydrated. Descents are best made at an aggressive pace in anticipation of the ice cold and magical ale awaiting you in the mystical Sedona refreshment zone (another guide in itself). Conversely, the winter chill may find you still sipping another cup of hot "C" before leaving your rig.

In summer, the upper reaches of Oak Creek Canyon (OCC) may provide a cool shady haven out of the sun, while the lower red rock portions of Oak Creek may put blisters on your blisters or just barely allow you to climb in the shade. In winter, the upper Coconino Sandstone portion of OCC may mimic the back of your Frigidaire, while in the sun, climbing might be crisp and classic. On the same day in winter, the lower red rock of OCC can be enchanting or the snow may be on you like white on rice. As a rule of thumb, Sedona is usually 10 degrees warmer than upper OCC, 15-20 degrees warmer than Flagstaff and 10-15 degrees cooler than Phoenix.

And now for a few words of warning: Beware of mid- to late-summer downpours which can bring flashfloods and gullywashers to red rock country, not to mention intense lightning. Keep a watchful eye for afternoon thunderstorm buildup and be prepared to bail out fast, i.e. leave gear. (What's a few bucks? If you're really hard up to sample a lightning strike, stick a wet hand into the back of your television.)

Also, brisk afternoon winds can make for their own brand of rapelling hell at any time of year. The best solution is to rappel with ropes coiled around your shoulders lest on a rock you be the wind's laughing stock! Some Sedona weather stats:

| | |
|---|---|
| Average summer temps: high: 90s low: 60s | As far as climbability goes: |
| Average winter temps: high: 50s low: 30s | October to mid-December: Primo! |
| Wettest months: July and Aug: 1.8-2.4 inches December and January 1.7 inches | Mid-December to March: Unpredictable, often quite nice. |
| Record Temperatures: high: 108 (July 1972) low: 0 (January 1968) | April to May. Exquisite, some gnats. |
| Record Snowfall: 35.2" (December 1967) | June to September: Poor to scorching. Choose alpine starts and shady routes. |
| Record Rainfall: 5.5" in one day (Sept. '70) | |

*Sweaty is sexy. Farrah Fawcett*     *Sweating is a waste of whiskey. Cowboy Expression*

---

# RATINGS

Route ratings follow the Yosemite Decimal System: 5.0 – 5.6= Beginning to easy technical rock climbing; 5.7 – 5.9= Intermediate; 5.10 – 5.12= Advanced to expert.

Bouldering ratings are approximate: B1 ~ 5.11+/12, B1+ ~ 5.12/13, B2 ~ 5.13.

Numbers have relatively little meaning here. Anyone can be far more afraid on routes two grades easier here than in other hard rock (e.g. granite) climbing areas.

The letter "R" after a rating denotes a lead fall which would raise reservations in a climber's mind and would probably result in unknown injury and/or increased sphincter size. The letter "X" means death or worse. In general, suffix all Sedona climbs with an "R" (guaranteed pain) or "X" (the ultimate penalty), knowing full well that at some point in the route you will not be able to trust the rock and/or your protection any further than you could toss your beefcake partner with a full aid rack on.

You may think by now I'm overplaying the scary side of Oak Creek climbing. But a lead of *Lucky Goes to the Creamery, Beeflord Spire,* or even a relatively safe route like *Dresdoom,* may slap you back into a cold sweat reality. In such cases, summit determination and commitment must be high. A first ascent bid usually (but not always) provides that "extra drive." Consequently, a second ascent party might find that "extra drive" has put them back in a nice safe lounge in town. Think about this: most first ascent parties would never go up on that route again. Although when asked face to face might exclaim, "It was a great route!" while staring at their feet and choking on their tongue.

# GEAR TO BRING

Wait, don't donate those old hexes to the museum yet! A well-slotted hex may save your day! But then, so could a toprope from a courageous partner. (When the going gets tough, the tough get some sucker to take the lead.) So, bring a brave partner, big culyôns, and the following: a standard rack with a double set of Friends, some hexes, set of wired stoppers, off-width pro, extra slings and knife for replacing dried rap anchors, and a bolt kit (baby angles and double expansion bolts may both work equally well). Wide crack or off-width conditions should be expected, thus big Friends are a must here as well for bar-room brawls. First ascensionists should be prepared for cleaning loose rock and the possibility of aid. And besides a fair amount of water and grub, a pair of tweezers may help the clumsy assuage cactus spines. (*I would fain die a dry death. Shakespeare, The Tempest Act 1, Sc. 2. I don't do Shakespeare. I don't talk in that broken kind of English. Mr. T.*)

Presently, Sedona sports one climbing shop. The closest other climbing emporiums are in Flagstaff. Phoenix and Prescott also have climbing shops. Check 'em out.

| | | |
|---|---|---|
| A5 Adventures | The Edge | Granite Mtn. Outfitters |
| 1109 S.Plaza Way #286 | 12 E Aspen | 320 W. Gurley St. |
| Flagstaff, AZ 86001 | Flagstaff, AZ 86001 | Prescott, AZ 86301 |
| (602)779-5084 | (602)774-4775 | (602)776-4949 |
| | | |
| Peace Surplus | Desert Mountain Sports | Go Take A Hike Sports |
| 14 W. Santa Fe | 2824 E Indian School Rd, #4 | 2730 W Highway 89A |
| Flagstaff, AZ 86001 | Phoenix, AZ 85016 | Sedona, AZ 86336 |
| (602)779-4521 | (602)955-2875 | (602)204-1171 |

## LOCAL INFO

In Sedona, excellent sources of local area info are:

US Forest Service
Coconino National Forest
Sedona Ranger Dist.
P.O. Box 300
Sedona, AZ 86336
(602)282-4119

Sedona Chamber of
Commerce
Forest Rd
Sedona, AZ 86336
(602)282-4119

Jeep Tour Companies
in uptown Sedona
Pink Jeep
Red Rock Jeep
Time Expeditions

This guidebook, heh heh…

If none of these good folks can help, you'll just have to do the best thing of all: explore on your own!

## RED ROCK CLIMBING TECHNIQUES

*[Warning: The Surgeon General has stated that rock climbing
in Sedona may be hazardous to your health.]*

To climb in Sedona is to know fear. I'm not talking about fear from being ten feet out from your last piece of protection, but rather the fear that comes from facing certain death. Because climbers visiting from "hard rock" areas will be wigging out, the following dos and don'ts are offered for your consideration and memory lapses:

*Don'ts:*

Don't fall! To fall on a route here is sheer stupidity. (Friends don't let friends fall on routes!)

Don't trust pro! Especially RPs. Runouts past foot level are ill-advised.

Don't trust holds! It's not a question whether the hold will break, but when. *[To worry is not to trust. To trust is not to worry.]*

*Dos:*

Do trust your mother when she tells you not to go climbing in Sedona.

Do trust a "bomber" Hex/nut over Friends/Tricams which can be dicey.

Do check the rock for hollow and loose conditions. Even *inside* cracks.

Do develop a sixth sense for soft rock. Experience will tell you what you can get away with, and experience comes slowly (or never again).

When climbing on loose holds: *["But it does move." Galileo before the Inquisition.]*

Do climb softly and lightly. Develop a light touch. Inhale helium.

Push ("glue") holds back in rather than pulling directly out (down). Palm stemming and mantling are effective.

Do remember: With the fragile nature of the rock, one climber's experience of a route may be different from a previous party's.

Do consult your life insurance agent.

Finally, if you ain't got a choice, be brave.

## RECOMMENDED ROUTES: None! (That was easy.)

Seriously though, recommending a route here is like handing a bottle of nitro to an epileptic friend. I would rather leave it up to your judgement. Still if you want suggestions, the route list and topos will help you get started.

*We can't leave the haphazard to chance. NF Simpson*

## FAVORITE ROUTES

While I won't recommend any routes, I will list a few which were either personally enjoyable or others have flipped over due to location, climbing, and/or summit views. Inclusion in this list does not mean they are safe routes or other great routes in the same grade do not exist.

4th Class – *Summit of Capitol Butte*

5.6 — *Chimney Rock, Courthouse Butte South Central Rib*

5.7 – *Streaker Spire, Queen Victoria*

5.8 – *Screaming Besingi, Bell Rock*

5.9 – *Dr. Rubo's Wild Ride, Epitaph, Coffee Pot Original Route, The Mace, Dresdoom*

5.10 – *Earth Angel, Princess Spire, Peter's Ladder, Book of Friends, The Big Corner*

5.11 – *Pointed Dome, Gunshy, Day in Court, Aladdin's Lamp, Coffee Pot South Face*

## RESCUE SERVICES

It use to be that if you got into a bind, it was sink or swim. You didn't expect the retirees in town to come after you. Now, the Sedona Fire Dept. has a professional rescue/climbing team available for emergency situations. Fortunately, they've been called for only one technical rescue to date. While this service costs the rescuee nothing, it does cost the taxpayer. The prevailing climbing attitude here should be: BYOR (Be Your Own Rescue)! In this soft rock, the Epic Potential (E.P.) is great. Like a good salad bar, it's really easy to create your own heaping epic. Climbers here should be able to rescue themselves both physically and emotionally. Some climbs are quite remote. Be sure to leave your whereabouts and last wishes with someone responsible. Leave your will and testament in care of the author. Sedona Fire Dept., 391 Forest Rd., Sedona, AZ 86336, (602)282-6800 Emergency: 911.

The Sedona Fire Dept. has been recognized as one of the country's outstanding fire departments. On April 22, 1989, their rescue team pulled off a record highline mock rescue by sending aloft warm-blooded "victim," Noel Caniglia 2,256 feet from the top of Teapot Rock down to Schnebly Hill Road on a single 2400', ½-inch rope (low stretch, of course). And she lived, now that's incredible!

In addition, Sedona is fortunate to have Ropes That Rescue, a leader in the field of emergency rescue instruction under the aegis of Reed Thorne. Ropes That Rescue, HC 30, Box 1121, Sedona, AZ 86336, (602)282-7299.

# CLIMBING HISTORY

Like history everywhere: some of it is well-known, some is obscure and difficult to obtain, some is slanted or changed, and some just plumb lost. Accordingly, Sedona's climbing history is varied, colorful and abundant. Until the last few years, the "scene" has always been somewhat transient in nature. Traveling climbers and the locals in Flagstaff would get *thoroughly* gripped on one, maybe two, routes during their stay. Then about a month to a year later, when fear had been forgotten, they'd anxiously return to have more "fun." Today, Sedona has attracted a small core of its own local climbers.

Presented here is a patented thumbnail sketch. Find other historical items (first ascentionists, tidbits, etc.) in the route list and topos. For a second helping, read *Rock & Ice* #21 pp.32-38 by Larry Coats.

**Pre-1950:** Man walks upright for years, then reverts to rock climbing.

**1950s:** Bob Kamps – first exploratory climbing, bags *The Mace* in '57 with TM Herbert, Dave Rearick. Does *Pointed Dome* and others.

**1960s:** Slow in Sedona. Overly preoccupied with first ascent to the Moon. Where's Fred Beckey when you need him?

**1970s(early):** The moon wanes, climbing shines in Sedona. Geoff Parker acquires Sedona fever – slays *Firecat, Streaker, Screaming Besingi,* etc. using the infamous "bong sandwich." "Mystery" bolt ladders discovered.

*Glen Rink featuring his down-home off-width gear on Damfino Spire.*

**1970s-early '80s:** Arizona Underground. Syndicato Granitico (the Alpineer lads) patrol the beat. A score of new routes, Scott Baxter and Ross Hardwick atop *Earth Angel, The Acropolis*; Larry and Tim Coats, Paul Davidson, Steve Grossman, hyperactive, establishing many classic and scary routes.

**1980s:** The New Age comes to Sedona. Many active Flagstaffians – Mike Lawson, Alex McGuffie, Chris Dunn, LB, etc.; Mish and Middendorf do *The Mushroom*. Sedona gets local scene, Fire Department organizes rescue/climbing team under Thorne. Visitors come from far and wide.

**1990s(late):** Sedona a nuclear waste dump. Freeze on new route activity. Climbing not recommended, rappel anchors questionable.

**2000s:** Fantastic sea cliff climbing! Reemergence of new activity. Buy a boat!

**3000s:** Ice climbing the rage. *Earth Angel* a 600' icicle. Chouinard moves shop to Sedona.

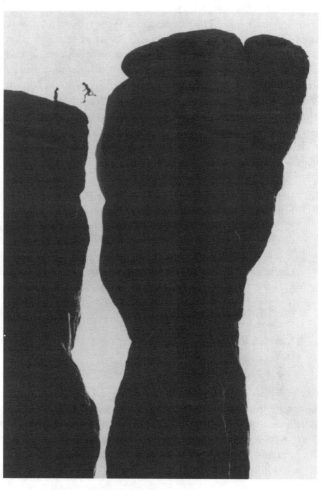

*Climbers on the timeless "jump-across" pitch on The Mace. Photo by: Jeff Bowman.*

While history is nice to know, it's more fun to make your own! So, back to the present.

*Great things happen when men and mountains meet.*
*This is not done while jostling in the street.*
William Blake

# HIKING AND BIKING TRAILS

The Sedona Ranger District manages approximately 52 system hiking trails. This guide mentions 29 of them. Please consult the Road Log and Climbing Maps for more specific info. Many of these trails were built by settlers in the late 1800s and early 1900s to provide canyon to rim access. All are beautiful hikes and usually rigorous and steep. For exploratory backpacking, Sycamore, Red Rock-Secret Mountain and Munds Mountain Wilderness Areas are three choice areas. When possible, use of trails for approaching climbs is highly recommended – to mitigate environmental and bodily injury.

For those needing to give their adrenal glands a rest, here are some recommended hikes:

Top 4 Rad Hikes

1. West Fork of Oak Creek #108: Requires a car shuttle to top of West Fork on Woody Mountain Road. Drops down east to Highway 89a. Strenuous, drops, pool crossings, big rock walls, bears.
2. North Wilson Trail #123: Nice elevation gain of 1700'. Stunning view of Sedona and Secret Canyon Wilderness.
3. A.B. Young Trail #100: A 2,000' elevation gain to East Pocket Lookout, Scenic Oak Creek Canyon vistas.
4. Secret Canyon Trail: Into the clandestine heart of Secret Canyon.

Top 4 Slacker Hikes

1. Parking lot into Oak Creek Tavern.
2. Devil's Kitchen Trail (from Soldier's Pass Trail): 75' elevation gain to 65' deep sinkhole.
3. Boynton Canyon Trail #47: Indian ruins and scenic beauty.
4. Sterling Pass Trail #46: Up to Vultee Arch.

For more info, see *A Guide to Exploring Oak Creek and the Sedona Area*, by Stewart Aitchison, 1989. *Sedona Guide Day Hiking and Sightseeing: Arizona's Red Rock Country* by Steve Krause and Teresa Hinkle 1991. Or, try *Sedona Hikes and Mountain Bike Rides* by Richard and Sherry Mangum 1992.

While some hiking trails are not suitable for mountain biking due to terrain or off-limits designation (wilderness areas), there is an array of varied and scenic mountain bike rides on jeep as well as hiking trails.

Top 5 Sedona Mountain Bike Rides

1. Schnebly Hill Road: Easier from east to west, i.e. downhill.
2. Midgely Bridge/Submarine Rock
3. Casner Canyon Trail: Desperate.
4. Submarine Rock-Broken Arrow Estates/Morgan Road: Not to be confused with Steamboat (Submarine Rock) at Midgely Bridge.
5. Dry Creek Road/Loy Butte FS 525

For more vivid details, see *Fat Tire Mountain Bike Book* by Cosmic Ray, 1994.

## CAMPING AND LODGING

*Eating and sleeping are a waste of time.*

Gerald R. Ford

Lodging: It's beyond the scope of this guide to list every choice of accommodation available. As there are nearly 54 hotels, etc. in the Sedona area, please call the Chamber of Commerce Hotline: (602)282-1117. Be aware that there is almost every kind of lodging available, from ultraposh to plush to scruff palace to terra firma.

Camping: Should you decide on mother earth, please be aware: in Oak Creek Canyon camping is only allowed in the five official USFS campgrounds from mid-May to mid-September with Pine Flat remaining open later. From north to south they are: Pine Flat, Cave Springs, Bootlegger, Banjo Bill, and Manzanita. Ten bucks a crack. If you want to escape this madness in summer, camping is free and abundant on Forest Service (not private) land north of the OCC Overlook and south of OCC around Sedona (e.g., Schnebly Hill Road or Dry Creek Road). Bring water.

## EATERIES AND FOOD ESTABLISHMENTS

*All sorrows are bearable if there is bread.*

Cervantes

The Sedona Business Profile says it in a mouthful, "Sedona is known for its plethora of excellent restaurants (about 60) to provide variety and to please even the most discriminating diner." If you're a rich climber, you now have a good excuse to back off that chosen choss pile. If you're poor, you'll have a lot of dishes to wash when it comes time to do something besides climb.

While it's never hard to find a restaurant around Sedona, these spots offer the climber a come-as-you-are, good value setting:

Breakfast – Coffee Pot Restaurant in west Sedona: Friendly service, 101 omelettes.

Novaki's – Good food in the Uptown Sedona bustle.

Mexican – Casa Miranda, west Sedona.

Italian – The Hideaway for an epicurean carbo-load, near the Market.

Thai – Thai Spices in west Sedona.

If you want to wear some snappy duds and be discriminating, try Garland's Lodge in OCC, but then, I'm biased (wink wink). It really is a gourmand's paradise.

## SEDONA PLANTS

[Note: Reading this section of the guide may save you the the money you forked out for it in skin damage alone. Hear me now, believe me later!]

In Sedona, the land forces the hiker to become a botanist. This is a simple task since there are only two classifications of plants to remember: plants that hurt, maim, and/or kill, and plants found elsewhere. Learn this now, because sooner or later, you are bound to "run" into one of them.

Non-voluntary plant identification is the least desirable form of plant taxonomy, but does proliferate an exciting vocabulary nonetheless. I was reminded of this the time I received a free two-inch cactus spine in my left shin during a dark descent back to the car. How can such brutality exist? Plants are beautiful, serene creatures, you say. The truth of the matter is that Sedona plants are anything but the peace-loving Easter lilies you may have grown to cherish as a child. Sedona plants are equipped with an arsenal that would send the Terminator on the run ("I von't be back.") They don't just attack singly, but in pairs and numbers, and they join forces with their cohorts in liaisons dangerous to climbers. It's a helpless feeling unknowingly working your way into a catclaw maze, sneaking by an Opuntia fence, only to face puncture by a yucca phalanx should you carelessly slip traversing a sandstone slab.

You don't like harming plants you say. Fine, I too, remember having that same benign attitude until one day I received an unexpected 360 degree lecture on the birds and the bees from a patch of catclaw acacia. That event permanently changed my outlook: I now step on catclaw. Frequently and with malice of forethought. Don't worry – they'll still live.

**A List of Plant Offenders**

| Hurt | Maim | Kill |
|---|---|---|
| Cactus spines (6 species) | Cactus spines | Yucca bayonets |
| Catclaw Acacia (rip) | Crucifixion Thorn | Agave spears |
| Poison Ivy (rash) | Catclaw Acacia | |
| Sotol (scratch) | New Mexican Locust | |
| Oak leaves (scratch) | Ocotillo | |
| Mesquite (poke) | | |
| Mountain mahogany (gouge) | | |

*In the desert sand, I could hear dry plants singing Lonely day and night. – Nelson Leonard*
I could add more but by now you get the point…so, why beat the bush? With these heinosities in mind, the following practices are recommended for a hurt/maim/death-free approach hike:

1. Don't fall down! A fall can mean a hand full of cactus glochids, an agave spike through the chest (pneumothorax) ala Ross Hardwick, or the ultimate penalty.

2. Review Rule #1.

3. Use stream beds, washes, gullies and ridges when possible for easiest walking. Hiking trails work well too.

4. Should you find yourself in the midst of battle in thick flesh-ripping brush, a controlled spinning motion will keep pokes and cuts to a minimum while providing an added dimension of fun to bushthrashing with such graceful dance steps as the Sotol Shuffle, Mimosa Minuet and the Yucca Two-Step.

5. Use your rucksack as a shield in fending off vegetation.

6. While it may sound destructive, stepping on plants may be the only effective way to get through the "jungle." The plants will remain unharmed.

7. The climb isn't finished until you reach your car. Often the hike in and out is the crux of the climb. Remember: Sucking on brews beats a sucking chest wound.

*Life is like licking honey off a cactus.*

# BIOLOGY

*Vita Celebratio Est (Life is a celebration.)*

Between Sedona and OCC, the diversity of natural life surrounding the climber is astounding. Biologists recognize six of the seven Merriam Life Zones. From the San Francisco Peaks (near Flagstaff) down to Phoenix they are: Zone 1 – Arctic, Zone 2 – Hudsonian, Zone 3 – Canadian, Zone 4 – Transition, Zone 5 – Upper Sonoran, and Zone 6 – Lower Sonoran. Tropical is Zone 7 and the only missing zone. The Transition and Upper Sonoran (woodland and grassland) are the main "zones" found in this guide. (The Peaks harbor Zones 1 to 3 and Phoenix Zone 6. Check Basha's banana section for Zone 7.)

Within these two zones, The Transition Zone 5 and Upper Sonoran Zone 5, biologists recognize eight different plant communities as shown here:

With all these different habitats, it's no wonder this area contains an abundance of life and a variety of species. Namely, 600 flowering plants, 58 mammals, 180 birds, 36 reptiles and amphibians, and 20 fishes (not to mention all the bugs and micro-life).

Standing atop the Overlook, you are in the largest Ponderosa Pine forest in the world! Down below, Oak Creek is an important riparian zone, a representative of only 0.001% of the Arizona land mass. Further still, the mouth of Oak Creek and the surrounding red rock benches offer you one of the few places on earth to view relict stands of Arizona Cypress trees. With so much diversity, this is truly a wonderland for natural historians.

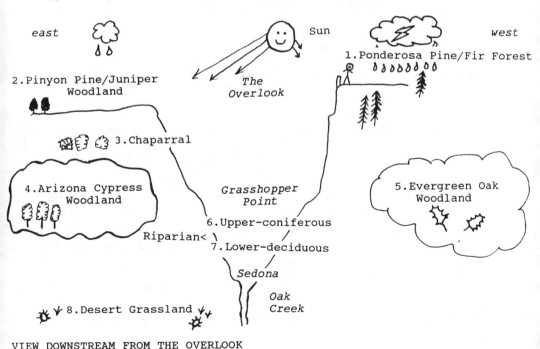

VIEW DOWNSTREAM FROM THE OVERLOOK

# GEOLOGY

As a climber, one cannot help but be enthralled by the surrounding geology. It is simply no less than fascinating. Although not quite as overwhelming as the Grand Canyon to the north, the geology is very similar. Learn one and you learn a lot about the other. The following thumbnail sketch and chart will hopefully give visiting climbers a quick appreciation for their surroundings. If you need a handful, please try " The Verde Valley: A Geologic History" *Plateau* Vol 60 #3 by Wayne Ranney; USGS Geologic Map of Sedona 30' x 60' Quadrangle by Weir, Ulrich, and Nealey, 1989; or the Northern Arizona University Geology Department.

Imagining the area as a 330 million year old sandstone/limestone layer cake (adding a little rum might help) with a toothbreaking basaltic frosting and you can begin to cut into the earth's secrets. The various layers or strata come from a variety of sediments deposited in a variety of environments.

In terms of geologic time, Oak Creek Canyon is still a young pup. While standing at the OCC Overlook, the Mogollon (pronounced "muggy-own," not "mongolloid") Rim stretched out before you is thought to have formed only 30-40 million years ago. Just 5 million years ago, the east block of the Oak Creek faultline (which follows Oak Creek) dropped 700 vertical feet in relation to the west block. The canyon itself is only 1 million years old...quite new when compared to the Grand Canyon of 10 million years. One other interesting observation: Oak Creek Canyon is much narrower than Dry Creek Canyon to the west, thought to be due in part to the rimline of basalt protecting the Oak Creek Canyon from erosion.

While Sedona's present setting offers astounding diversity, a quick perusal of the rock record reveals far more. Consider that in the 300 million years of geologic history that one can view from Pointed Dome, this area has donned all the following environmental faces: tropical seas, marine deltas, river floodplains, tidal flats, desert sand dunes, and even volcanoes. Not bad for 25 square miles, eh?

Of the rock layers climbers touch, the following five layers are used most frequently.

| | | |
|---|---|---|
| Tertiary Basalt | 15 mya<br>(million years ago) | columnar crack climbing areas (e.g. Oak Creek Waterfall) |
| Kaibab Limestone | 250 mya | sport climbing and bouldering (e.g. Le Petit Verdon, Priest Draw in Flagstaff) |
| Coconino Sandstone | 260 mya | large (400 ft) tan Oak Creek Canyon/Sedona Walls (e.g. Coke Wall) |
| Schnebly Hill Formation | 265 mya | all Sedona Red Rock Buttes and Spires (e.g. The Mace, Steamboat Rock, et al) |
| Supai Group | 285 mya | inner gorge of Oak Creek Canyon bouldering / topropes (e.g. Grasshopper Point) |

*Sand drums of the desert…*
*Traveler of the desert sand…*
*They travel in the wind,*
*In wind travels the land.*
Ronald King

*Earth Angel Spire showcased from the air*

# CLIFF DWELLINGS, ROCK ART, AND HISTORY, ETC.

En route to the base of your climb, you may chance upon cliff dwellings and/or pictographs. Lo and behold, ancient cultures have been digging the scenery in these parts long before the three million visitors to OCC in the 1990s. Sitting near a cliff dwelling on a calm spring day, one can easily see how the amicable climate would appeal to the prehistoric Sinagua culture and the historic Yavapai/Apache people. Archaeologists have been trying to piece together this puzzle of humanity for some time now. With many questions still to be answered, the following represents the bare bones of their findings:

8000 BC – AD 1: Dry Creek Phase. First definite evidence of human presence, e.g. projectile points, small manos, metates, and stone flakes.

AD 1 – 700: Sinagua Culture and the beginning of agriculture. Sinagua (Spanish "without water") first permanent residents and "dry farmers" rely on rainfall rather than irrigation.

AD 700 – 1000: Hohokam Influence. Sinagua adapt Hohokam (a prehistoric Phoenician group) irrigation techniques, become adept mesa top farmers, social organization and trade centers evolve.

AD 1000 – 1125: Consolidation Phase. Family size and social relations become stabilized, Hohokam influence peaks.

AD 1130 – 1300: Honanki Phase. General expansion due to rise in moisture; construction and occupation of red rock cliff dwellings in western Sedona. Honanki dwellings at Loy Butte, Palatki dwellings near Red Canyon; Tuzigoot phase evolving.

AD 1300 – 1400: Great Pueblo Phase. Multistoried structures at Montezuma's Castle and Tuzigoot. The golden age for southern Sinagua; active pottery trade as far as Winslow/Hopi Mesa, agave a major food source.

AD 1425 – ?: Great Mystery Phase: Sinagua abandon Verde Valley by 1425. This is perhaps the biggest question mark in local archaeology. Suggested theories include the usual – drought, warfare, disease – religion, perhaps merged with now local Yavapai tribe. Or the climber's hypothesis: they heard about better climbing in places like Joshua Tree and Yosemite Valley. Anyway, the question remains: Why this void at the apex of living conditions, farming technology, sophisticated political and social systems, and "trade routes" (not to mention all those unclimbed spires and buttes)?

AD 1400 – 1800: Yavapai and Apache fill the gap in Sinagua disappearance; nomadic hunters and food gatherers with keen wild plant and animal knowledge (100+ species). Agave an important food source, expert basketmakers, pictograph artists of Red Canyon, frequent Boynton Canyon red rock country.

AD 1871 – 1873: War of attrition with Gen. George Crook. Herded onto reservations.

For better insight of these ancient cultures, a trip to Montezuma's Castle/Montezuma's Well (just south of Sedona, east off I-17) or Tuzigoot National Monument (east of Clarkdale) is recommended.

*In spite of the cost of living, it's still popular. Kathleen Norris*

A SPECIAL NOTE: Cliff dwellings and pictographs are protected under the Archaeological Protection Act of 1979. Please walk as softly on the land as did these ancient cultures. Leave these public treasures as you found them…unless of course it's a huge pot worth millions, give me a call.

A few more bits of general history:

1583: Antonio de Espejo, first non-Indian in area, finds Indian copper mines rather than sought after gold.

1598: Spaniard Marcos de los Godos coins term Cruzados (people with crosses) for Yavapai's headwear.

1860s: Capt. Joseph Walker and other pioneers become first Anglo-Americans in area.

1902-30: Sedona Post Office established. Named after postmaster Schnebly's wife cuz his name was too long for postal stamp. Schools and roads developed.

## A VORTEX TOUR

Climbers ascending the red rock formations in this guide may have already been among the famed Sedona Vortices and not even known it. A vortex is a natural power or energy spot on the earth. This energy is measurable through electronic instruments. The force transmitted to a person standing in the area can have varying affects. A vortex is classed in one of three ways according to its charge:

Electric – positive charge (male): Charges the body and emotions, elevates consciousness.

Magnetic – negative (female): Makes one more receptive, perceptive and in tune to the inner-self.

Electromagnetic – balanced charge, a force field: A relationship of one's own energy to the earth's.

Sedona lays claim to having the largest concentration of vortices of any place on earth. (The numbers vary as more become known). This has made the area a mecca for a large body of metaphysical and holistic folks. In 1987, a Harmonic Convergence ceremony was held in which 5,000 people came together with a desire to heal a hurting planet. This quest arose from the theory that the earth is a living body having unique emotions and feelings—a vortex then is the earth's emotional response to its evolutional development. All vortices have been denoted with a "V" on the general area map. (This information was derived from vortex expert, Page Bryant's tape *The Sedona Vortices*.)

Eight Vortices of Sedona

1.  Cathedral Rock (magnetic): Extends for 500' around the base, affects the subconscious mind.

2.  Airport Mesa (electric): Most well-known. Great for depression and higher levels of consciousness; not recommended for people with heart problems.

3.  Boynton Canyon (electromagnetic): The largest and most powerful in Sedona, stimulates creativity; sacred to Yavapai – Home of Great Mother.

Hmm, Great place for a Post Office

4. Bell Rock (electric): Lifts consciousness; the "Beacon Vortex" to call other planets, sacred to Yavapai – Home of the Eagle.
5. Apache Leap (magnetic): Cliffs across road from Bell Rock. The only negative vortex. As yet no climbing routes have been done.
6. Hill behind US Post Office: Only time warp vortex; causes temporary confusion, disorientation.
7. Indian Gardens: A manmade vortex in OCC, dies out unless constantly recharged (humans are vortices). Stonehenge is another example.
8. Medicine Wheel: Another manmade vortex west of Merry-Go-Round Rock on Schnebly Hill Road. The largest medicine wheel in this area.

In your ramblings, you may notice a circle of stones, like the illustration to the right. These are known as medicine wheels/energy circles.

Enuff said for now, as your undertaker, I suggest you prepare your will and pick your pallbearers wisely as you join me for a journey into the macabre…

*Think wrongly, if you please, but in all cases think for yourself. Lissing*

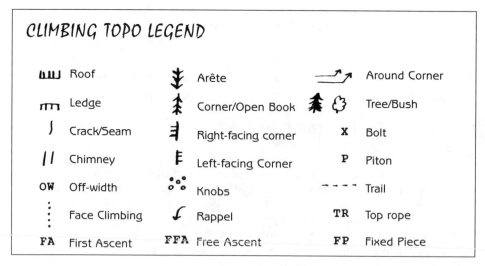

## CLIMBING TOPO LEGEND

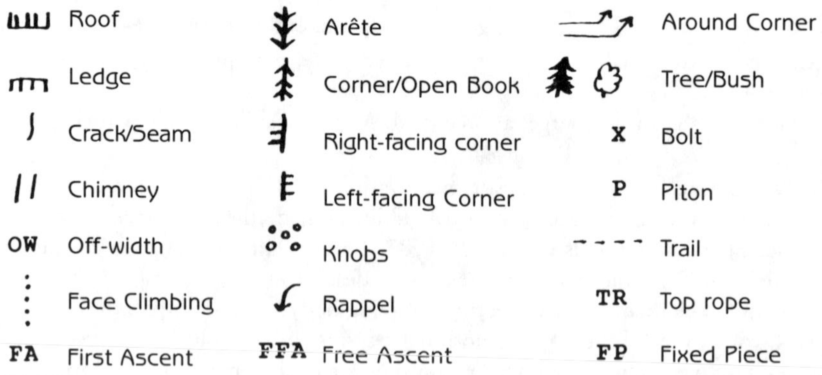
Roof
Ledge
Crack/Seam
Chimney
OW Off-width
Face Climbing
FA First Ascent
Arête
Corner/Open Book
Right-facing corner
Left-facing Corner
Knobs
Rappel
FFA Free Ascent
Around Corner
Tree/Bush
X Bolt
P Piton
Trail
TR Top rope
FP Fixed Piece

Topos are listed in the same direction as the climbs in the Route List. Roman numerals next to the rating refers to the grade as follows:

I=one hour climb; II=half a day; III=most of the day; IV=a long full day

No grade fives (overnighters) exist in Sedona yet, except those brought about unwillingly by climbers, a.k.a., an epic.

# CLIMBER'S ROAD LOG

Below is a handy list of mileposts to assist the climber in finding formations and parking areas to access them. Road Log Abbreviations: >=to L=left R=right N=north(S,W,E) mi=miles CG=campground HT=hiking trail~=approximately Jct=road junction *P=parking area to depart for climbs. To locate an area, use the green milepost markers along the highway when available. Your odometer readings may vary slightly between milepost markers. All mileages are correct give or take 0.2 mi due to DWI (Driving While Interpolating).

## CLIMBER'S ROAD LOG – AREAS A THROUGH F&M; B1 THROUGH B3

| FLAGSTAFF>OAK CREEK CANYON | | |
|---|---|---|
| | MILES . . .MILEPOST | |
| Jct I-40 and I-17 | 0.0 | |
| Jct Hwy 89A and I-17(Airport exit) | 2.6 . . .398.9 | |
| *P- Upper Pumphouse Wash (~3/4mi E on dirt rd ) | . . . .390.7 | |
| *P-Oak Creek Overlook | 11.5 . . .390 | |
| Oak Creek Faultline to N | . . . .388.9 | |
| *Faults are the easiest things to find* | | |
| *P-Lower Pumphouse Wash (bridge) | . . . .387.7 | |
| Spring Water>W;Cookstove Hiking Trail(HT) to (>)East | . . . .386.8 | |
| *P-Pine Flat CG (Grim Reaper) | 14.8 . . .386.7 | |
| Richard's Buttress /Kaibab Cap View>W | . . . .386 | |
| *P-Troutdale Ranch/Cave Springs CG Harding Springs HT>E | . . . .385.8 | |
| Book of Friends/Dresdoom (view>NE) | . . . .385.4 | |
| USFS Picnic Area | . . . .384.6 | |
| *P-West Fork of Oak Creek HT>W and Thomas Point HT>E | 17.1 . . .384.4 | |
| Coke Wall | . . . .384.2 | |
| *P-W of Don Hoel's Cabin >Coke Wall | . . . .383.6 | |
| *P-Bootlegger CG/AB Young HT>W | . . . .383.1 | |
| Basalt dike on left | . . . .383 | |
| Junipine Resort | . . . .382.9 | |
| Banjo Bill CG/Garland's Lodge | . . . .382.6 | |
| Halfway Picnic Ground | . . . .382.0 | |
| *P-Slide Rock Bouldering>W | . . . .381.7 | |
| View of bathing beauties | . . . .381.5 | |

| *P-Slide Rock State Park | 20.3 . . .381.2 | |
|---|---|---|
| Natural Arch/Sandcastles (view>W) | . . . .381 | |
| Sterling Pass HT>with Manzanita CG | . . . .380.5 | |
| *P-Waterfall Area (basalt-high>E) | . . . .379.6 | |
| Encinoso Picnic Area/ N Wilson Mtn HT | . . . .379.4 | |
| Thompson's Ladder HT | . . . .378.6 | |
| Indian Gardens/Mund's Cyn>E | . . . .378.2 | |
| Views of Red Rocks>S; Flying Buttress> Pointed Dome from E>W | . . . .377 | |
| Casner Canyon HT>E | . . . .376.9 | |
| *P-Grasshopper Point (.3mi>boulders) Allen's Bend HT | 24.8 . . .376.7 | |
| *P-Midgley Bridge/ Submarine Rock> W Wilson Cyn and S Wilson Mtn HT's>N | . . . .376.1 | |
| Green Sedona Sign;View>S of Camelhead, BJ Rock, Lost Chapel Area and Cathedral Rock from E>W | . . . .375.2 | |
| *P-Anvil Rock Bouldering>E | . . . .375 | |
| Jct Hwy 89A(OC Tavern) and Jordan Rd (N~1.3mi) to *P-Earth Angel Area | 374.5 | |
| Sedona Fire Dept/ Commerce Chamber | . . . .374.4 | |
| Jct Hwy 179 and Hwy 89A | 27.3 . . .374.2 | |

## CLIMBER'S GUIDE AREAS G, H, I

| HWY 179 & HWY 89A> SCHNEBLY HILL RD & I17 | MILES |
|---|---|
| Jct Hwy 179 and Hwy 89A | 0.0 |
| Hwy 179andSchnebly Hill Rd | 0.4 |
| pavement meets dirt | 0.9 |
| alt*P-Slingshot Rock (see Marg's Draw) | 1.0 |
| View of Damfino Spire (skyline notch/corner) | 1.6 |
| *P-Damfino Spire (roadbend on S) | 1.9 |
| *P-Pointed Dome | 2.2 |
| *P-Thumb's Up | 2.5 |
| *P-Schnebly Hill South Area and Flying Buttress | 3.1 |
| Merry-Go-Round Rock on left | 5.1 |
| *P-Schnebly Hill Overlook (Basalt)>N | 6.8 |
| FS Road 801 (S~4mi> Munds Mtn HT | ~8.7 |
| I-17 and Schnebly Hill Rd. Exit | 12.6 |
| Jct Hwy 89A and I-17 (Flagstaff Airport Rd) | 29.9 |

## CLIMBER'S ROAD LOG AREA K

| HWY 179 AND JACKS CYN RD>OC SPIRES | MILES |
|---|---|
| Jct Hwy 179 and Jacks Cyn Rd>E | 0.0 |
| Jct with Lee Mtn Rd(go R) | 0.9 |
| *P-USFS Access(gate)/ Jacks Cyn HT: N>OC Spire | 2.7 |
| Pine Valley Estates[private] | 2.7+100' |

## CLIMBER'S ROAD LOG AREAS I, J, K, L, B4

| JCT HWY 179 AND HWY 89A. MACE/OC SPIRE/I-17 | Miles | Mile Marker |
|---|---|---|
| Jct Hwy 179 and Hwy 89A | 0.0 | . . .313.7 |
| Jct Hwy 179 and Schnebly Hill Rd. | | . . . . .313.1 |
| Sombart Ln at Circle K (E for 0.2mi> *P-Marg's Draw Area) | 0.9 | . . .312.8 |
| Morgan Rd (~1/2mi E>*P-Devil's Dining Room sinkhole-1/2mi hike) | 1.6 | . . .312.1 |
| Chavez Crossing | | . . . .311.4 |
| Chapel Hill Rd (E 0.8 mi> *P-Church Spires Area) | 2.9 | . . .310.8 |
| Back-O-Beyond Rd (W 0.7mi> pullout on L *P-Cathedral Spires(for Mace) | 3.5 | . . .310.2 |
| *P-Bell Rock (E pullout) | | . . .308.1 |
| *P-Danny's Boulders (S of cattleguard) | 5.8 | . . .307.9 |
| Bell Rock Blvd/Circle K | | . . .307.1 |
| Jacks Cyn Rd (see log below) and Verde Valley School Rd (W ~4.1mi to *P-Westside Cathedral Rocks) | 7.3 | . . .306.4 |
| Woods Cyn/Hot Loop HT | 8.9 | . . .304.8 |
| Graben(faultline) | 10.6 | . . .303.1 |
| I-17 | 14.8 | . . .298.9 |

## CLIMBER'S ROAD LOG AREAS N, O, P

| WEST SEDONA(89A)>COTTONWOOD . | MILES | MILEPOST |
|---|---|---|
| Jct Hwy 89A and Hwy 179 | 0.0 | . . .374.2 |
| US Post Office | | . . . .374 |
| Airport Rd on left (S 0.4mi view) | 1.1 | . . .373.1 |
| Soldier Pass Rd (N~1.0mi>Cline Dr>W | 1.3 | . . .372.9 |
| *P-Summit Block;OR ~2.0 mi to Rim Shadows Dr and USFS access *P-Coffee Pot, Japhead Devil's Kitchen/ Soldier Pass HTs Andante Dr [Circle K]- (N ~1.1 mi to Skyview Way>*P -Chimney Rock, T-Rex,etc | 2.6 | . . .371.6 |
| Dry Creek Rd | 3.2 | . . .371 |
| Upper Red Rock Loop Rd | 4.3 | . . .369.9 |
| Lower Red Rock Loop Rd | 5.6 | . . .368.6 |
| Loy Canyon Rd | 9.7 | . .~364.5 |
| Jct Hwy 89A and Hwy 279(Cottonwood) | 19.0 | . .~354.8 |

## CLIMBER'S ROAD LOG
## AREA P

DRY CREEK RD>STERLING
  CANYON

| | |
|---|---|
| Jct Hwy 89A and Dry Creek Rd | 0.0 |
| Dry Creek Rd(ROCKY!/dirt) cutoff 52C N> Sterling Canyon | 2.0 |
| Devil's Bridge (arch) cutoff (0.4 miE> D Bridge HT) | 3.4 |
| Brins Mesa (Soldier Pass) HT>E | 4.6 |
| Secret Cyn HT>W | 5.6 |
| Dry Creek Cyn HT | 6.4 |
| *P-Sterling Cyn HT-E> Vultee Arch (deadend) | 6.5 |

DRY CREEK RD>
  LONG CANYON RD(152D)MILES

| | |
|---|---|
| Jct Hwy 89A and Dry Creek Rd | 0.0 |
| Dry Creek Rd (dirt cutoff) | 2.0 |
| Jct Long Canyon Rd(right) and Boynton Pass Rd(152)(left) | 2.8 |
| *P-Long Canyon HT>W | 3.5 |
| Long Cyn Rd end(great viewpoint) | 4.5 |

CT BOYNTON PASS RD
  and LONG CYN RD>

FAY CYN ARCH/LOY BUTTE
  MILEAGE

| | |
|---|---|
| Jct BPR(152) and LCR(152D) past jeep trail and cattleguard | 0.0 |
| Jct BPR and Boynton Cyn Rd (N 0.3mi to *P-Boynton Cyn HT and Gardiner's Enchantment Resort) | 1.7 |
| *P-Fay Canyon HT (Arch) | 2.3 |
| Doe Mtn.(on left) | ~2.7 |
| Boynton Pass | ~2.9 |
| 152A to Cockscomb Spires (S~3mi on rough dirt road a.k.a. "The Cockscomb Highway") | 4.9 |
| Jct 152 and 525 N>Loy Butte (S back to Hwy 89A ~5.8mi) | 5.8 |
| Red Canyon Cutoff | 6.0 |
| Hartwell Canyon | 8.2 |
| *P-Loy Canyon HT (deadend) | ~9.5 |

*At the crux on Princess Spire*

# BOULDERING AREAS

Wending south from Oak Creek Overlook, four areas present the boulderer his fix. Besides these four areas, other sporadic and worthy boulders may be found along Oak Creek's streambed and in the Sedona backcountry for bouldering pioneers. On the whole, sandstone boulders tend to be slippery with unreliable holds, making one hesitant to get too high off the deck without a good insurance policy. Solid basalt boulders that fall from the rim like manna from heaven are the exception, e.g., "Dick's Bowling Ball," and something to be sought after by the would-be boulderer. From north to south:

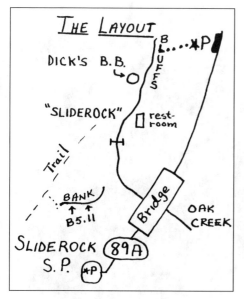

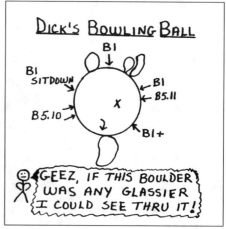

**B1**   **Slide Rock State Park:** Bouldering can be found at Dick's Bowling Ball, a creekside basalt boulder north of the "slide" at Slide Rock waterplay area. This is probably the best single boulder yet discovered in Oak Creek Canyon. Credit Dick Cilley with the problems on the Bowling Ball. A few other good problems lie just below the slide on river right on a 12' sandstone wall. There are also short topropes on the walls upstream from Dick's.

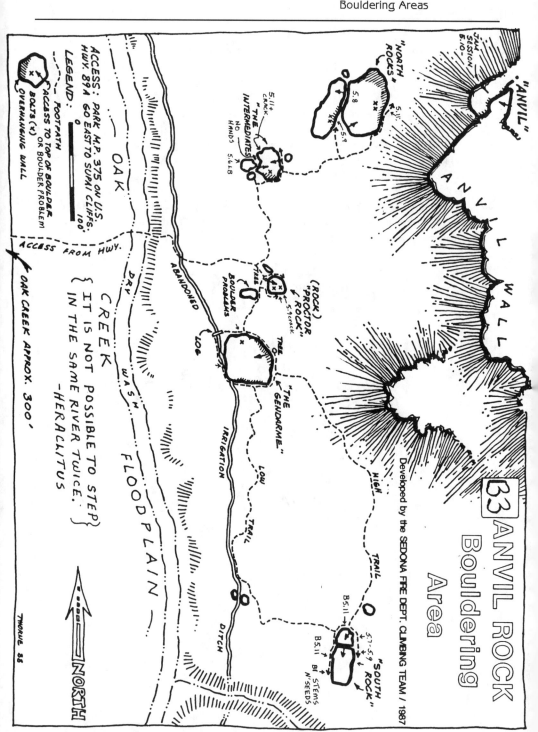

B3 ANVIL ROCK Bouldering Area

Developed by the SEDONA FIRE DEPT. CLIMBING TEAM / 1987

"ANVIL"

ANVIL WALL

"NORTH"

"NORTH ROCKS"

JAM SESSION 5.10

5.8

5.9

5.11 CRACK

"THE INTERMEDIATES"

NO HANDS 5.6.1.8

OAK

LEGEND:
ACCESS TO TOP OF BOULDER

ACCESS TO TOP OF BOULDER OR BOULDER PROBLEM
BOLTS (X)
OVERHANGING WALL

----- Footpath

ACCESS: PARK M.P. 375 ON U.S. HWY. 89A  GO EAST TO SUPAI CLIFFS.

100'

ACCESS FROM HWY.

OAK CREEK APPROX. 300'

DRY WASH

ABANDONED

BOULDER PROBLEMS

TRAIL

LOG

(ROCK) "PROCTOR ROCK"
5.3 CRACK

"THE GENDARME"

CREEK
{ IT IS NOT POSSIBLE TO STEP IN THE SAME RIVER TWICE. }
—HERACLITUS

FLOOD PLAIN

IRRIGATION

LOW TRAIL

DITCH

HIGH TRAIL

B5.11

B5.11    5.7-5.9

B5.11    STEMS N' SEEDS

"SOUTH ROCK"

THORNE 88

NORTH

**B2** Grasshopper Point: "G.P." holds lots of good exploration. On the rock, and on the beach. These steep, solid, and fairly extensive bluffs lining Oak Creek are most suited to short toprope problems. The Midgely Bridge Area, further downstream, is closed by the Forest Service due to visitor safety.

**B3** Anvil Rock: Anvil Rock sports the most extensive concentration in Sedona for good boulder problems of all grades. Tall, though somewhat sandy blocks lie across the creek from North Sedona. See aerial map by Reed Thorne on page 25.

**B4** Danny's Boulder: A classic 5.9 handcrack on 35' block in the drainage west-southwest of Bell Rock. Park just south of cattleguard and walk west-southwest to this streambed boulder. The undaunted will not need a rope nor four or five handcrack-sized Friends.

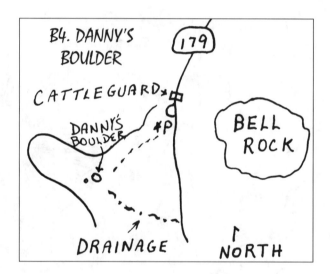

## THOUGHTS FROM A BACKCOUNTRY CLIMB

It's been a long climb so far and by now you're just wanting to get it over with…Weltering in sweat, mouth dry and dusty, you feel like an elephant with a stubbed toe. Breaths come hard as your legs strain to overcome the gravity of steep red rock. Gingerly, you tiptoe by a cactus playing ledge Monopoly. One bad roll now and the rest of your day could be painless. Fortunately, you pass GO.

Another move up and the rock crumbles beneath your feet, floating shards into space. Fifty feet further, an agave threatens to put you between a rock and a hard spot. You stand up on some dubious blocks pulling hard to reach the next set of good holds. It was a pretty good crank (maybe 5.10, eh?). Pausing to catch your breath, you notice you would've pincushioned flat onto a cactus had the blocks departed…at least the ledge it lay on would've stopped you from falling hundreds of feet, heh heh. You endure it though, knowing soon it'll all be worth it.

Almost there now…one last unprotected traverse. What a setting! Exposure rivals view. Hopefully your partner will make it! A stray mahogany pushes you away from the wall, conjuring up the question: what's pumping harder, forearms or adrenal glands? A few more moves on some mank rock and CONGRATULATIONS! Take off that pack…you've just made a typical approach to the base of another climb in the Sedona outback!

*On pitch 2 of Dr Rubo's Wild Ride, Summit Block Rock*

# OAK CREEK CANYON/SEDONA ROUTE LIST

Route descriptions are given as one faces the rock. The compass direction in which the routes are described is given next to the area's name. When possible, each description includes route name, rating, first ascent team, date, number of pitches, and routefinding notes. Names of first ascentists are used once then abbreviated.

## A. PUMPHOUSE WASH

These routes lie in the canyon east of Oak Creek Overlook. Described from north (upper) to south (lower).

1.  **Unnamed  A2** [Rand Black, Todd Applewhite 1986.] One pitch 90' on east-side white wall at bottom of hike-down upper Pumphouse Wash.

2.  **Saved by Zero A3** [T. Applewhite, R. Black 1986.] One pitch. Left-facing corner 30' feet right of Unnamed (Route 1).

3.  **Feed the Fish A4** [T. Applewhite, R. Black 1986.] One pitch. Left-facing corner 20' farther right of Saved by Zero, above pond(a grim swim).

4.  **Ultimate Finger Crack 5.11+** [Tim Coats, John Mattson 1985.] One pitch. On right below beaver pond. This 150' face-splitting crack lies in the dark corridor between two white buttresses. Unique.

5.  **Unnamed 5.11-** [Jim Haisley, P. Davidson 1985.] One pitch. Dihedral behind Ultimate Finger Crack in back of alcove. Good.

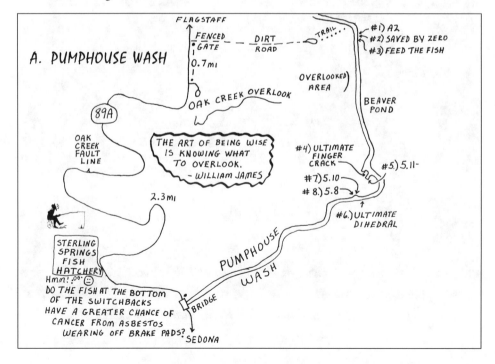

6. **Ultimate Dihedral 5.11-** [T.Coats, Stan Mish 1985.] Three pitches. Right-facing corner. Mossy start with baby angle pitons. Worthy sustained first pitch. Located downstream and around bend on left from Ultimate Finger Crack.

7. **Unnamed 5.10** [Steve Grossman, Paul Davidson mid-1980s.] Two-pitch, 100' handcrack across from Ultimate Dihedral. Needs bolt and belay anchors.

8. **Unnamed 5.8** [T.Coats, J.Haisley mid-1980s.] One pitch. 60' handcrack just left of Ultimate Finger Crack.

# B. ALONG OAK CREEK CANYON

Starting at the bottom of the switchbacks, routes are described on the west side of Highway 89A from north to south.

1. **King Tut 5.10R/X** [P. Davidson, J.Haisley early '80s.] Two to three pitches. Routes #1 and #2 from drainage west of Pine Flat Campground. Lies on north side of drainage, obvious corner on left of broad face. Pitch 1: Corner to 25' traverse to tree. Pitch 2: Corner to bush to overhang.

2. **Grim Reaper 5.10R** [T.Coats, P.Davidson 1980] Three pitches. First obvious fin/spire with little roofs on south side of drainage, west of Pine Flat Campround. Start at bottom of prow. Pitch 1: 5.8 face. Pitch 2: 5.10 Left-leaning crack to southwest face to ledge. Pitch 3: 5.9 face on prow, 1 rappel off north to walk-off on east-side summit block.

Grim Reaper

Grim Reaper from Pine Flats CG

3. **Richard's Ladder 5.11+ A1** [P. Davidson, Scott Baxter, T.Coats, Mark Peterson 1978-81.] Four pitches. Prominent orange buttress split by obvious dogleg crackline. Pitch 1:5.8. Pitch 2: 5.11+ hands to offwidth. Pitch 3: 5.11X A1 dogleg(clip pin then from belay ledge traverse left to arête to vertical-aid at top. Pitch 4: 5.9 20' face. Scarewee.

4. **Kaibab Cap 5.8** [Roma Ramblers 1962. Fourth class west face by Alpineer lads 1980s.] One pitch. East face. Obvious high white-twinned tower south (left) and above *Richard's Ladder.*

Kaibab Cap

Richard's Ladder

Kaibab Cap and Richard's Ladder from US 89A

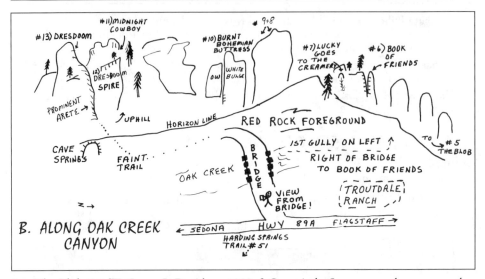

5. **The Blob 5.9** [T. Coats, P. Davidson 1980s.] One pitch. Starts around corner north of Book of Friends. North of big cave on ramp to left-facing finger dihedral. Tree rappel.

6. **Book of Friends 5.10** [S. Baxter, John Gault 1979.] Three pitch. Obvious big orange book. Classic off-width and chimney. Rappel from tree 100 yards to south.

7. **Lucky Goes to the Creamery 5.11X** [S. Grossman, P. Davidson, J. Haisley, T. Coats 1980s.] Three pitches. Arête 200' south of Book of Friends. Pitch 1: Corner/lieback, two bolts. Pitch two: 5.8 face to square chimney to arête. Pitch 3: Arête. Needs two bolts?. Rappel same as *Book of Friends*. Serious route. No joking.

8. **Keenies Korner 5.10R** [P. Davidson, T. Coats 1981.] One pitch. Black left-leaning corner/stem. Starts from a dead tree at a rounded corner/ridge south of *Book of Friends*.

Dresdoom / Book of Friends Area from just west of Troutdale Ranch, West of 89A

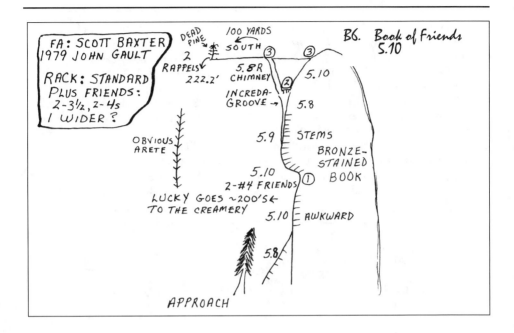

FA: SCOTT BAXTER
1979 JOHN GAULT

RACK: STANDARD
PLUS FRIENDS:
2-3½, 2-4s
1 WIDER?

DEAD PINE

100 YARDS
SOUTH

2 RAPPELS
222.2'

5.8R
CHIMNEY

INCREDA-GROOVE →

OBVIOUS ARETE

5.9

5.10
2-#4 FRIENDS

LUCKY GOES ~200'S ←
TO THE CREAMERY

5.10  AWKWARD

5.8

APPROACH

B6.  *Book of Friends*
5.10

③      ③

②
5.10

5.8

STEMS

BRONZE-STAINED BOOK

①

---

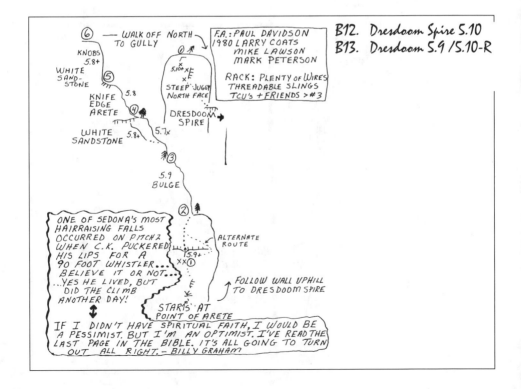

⑥ — WALK OFF NORTH
TO GULLY

KNOBS
5.8+

WHITE SAND-STONE

⑤

KNIFE EDGE ARETE

④

5.8

5.8+

WHITE SANDSTONE

5.7x

③

5.9 BULGE

②

F.A.: PAUL DAVIDSON
1980 LARRY COATS
MIKE LAWSON
MARK PETERSON

RACK: PLENTY OF WIRES
THREADABLE SLINGS
TCU's + FRIENDS > #3

Ø

5.10+

STEEP 'JUGGY'
NORTH FACE

DRESDOOM SPIRE →

ALTERNATE ROUTE

ONE OF SEDONA'S MOST
HAIRRAISING FALLS
OCCURRED ON PITCH 2
WHEN C.K. PUCKERED
HIS LIPS FOR A
90 FOOT WHISTLER...
BELIEVE IT OR NOT...
...YES HE LIVED, BUT
DID THE CLIMB
ANOTHER DAY!

5.9+
XX ①

FOLLOW WALL UPHILL
TO DRESDOOM SPIRE

STARTS AT
POINT OF ARETE

IF I DIDN'T HAVE SPIRITUAL FAITH, I WOULD BE
A PESSIMIST. BUT I'M AN OPTIMIST. I'VE READ THE
LAST PAGE IN THE BIBLE. IT'S ALL GOING TO TURN
OUT ALL RIGHT. — BILLY GRAHAM

B12.  *Dresdoom Spire* 5.10
B13.  *Dresdoom* 5.9 /5.10-R

9. **Mudrat 5.10** [P. and Peggy Davidson 1980s.] Three pitches. Flat face right around corner from *Burnt Bohemian Buttress*.

10. **Burnt Bohemian Buttress 5.10** [J. Haisley, P. Davidson early '80s.] Two to three pitches. Obvious off-width crack on white buttress. Pitch 1: 5.10 40' face. Pitch 2: 80' squeeze chimney. Good.

11. **Midnight Cowboy 5.10+X** [P. Davidson, etal early '80s.] One pitch. Slanting face with pin at start. Traverse to knobs (use #4 Friend and rope lasso—bolt needed) to headwall in notch-wall to right of *Dresdoom Spire*.

12. **Dresdoom Spire 5.10+** [T. Coats, Jim Haisley 1985.] One pitch. Starts above Dresdoom on overhanging juggy face. Three drilled angles for protection. Good.

13. **Dresdoom 5.9+/5.10-R** [P. Davidson, Larry Coats, Mark Peterson, Mike Lawson. First continuous ascent 1980.] Six pitches. Two-tiered red to white aesthetic arête. Frighteningly classique.

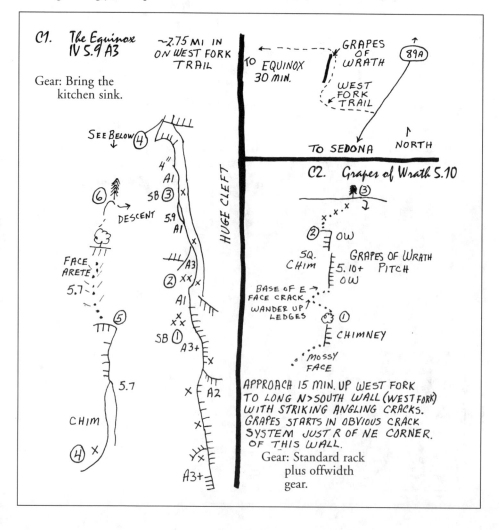

C1. The Equinox IV 5.9 A3

~2.75 MI IN ON WEST FORK TRAIL

TO EQUINOX 30 MIN.

GRAPES OF WRATH

89A

WEST FORK TRAIL

TO SEDONA    NORTH

Gear: Bring the kitchen sink.

SEE BELOW 4

4" AI
SB 3 X
DESCENT 5.9 AI

6

FACE ARETE 5.7

A3
2 XX X
AI
XX
SB 1
A3+

5

5.7

CHIM

4 X

HUGE CLEFT

A2

A3+

C2. Grapes of Wrath 5.10

3
x . x . x
2 OW

SQ. CHIM
GRAPES OF WRATH 5.10+ PITCH
OW

BASE OF E FACE CRACK
WANDER UP LEDGES
3 1

CHIMNEY

MOSSY FACE

APPROACH 15 MIN. UP WEST FORK TO LONG N>SOUTH WALL (WEST FORK) WITH STRIKING ANGLING CRACKS. GRAPES STARTS IN OBVIOUS CRACK SYSTEM JUST R OF NE CORNER OF THIS WALL.

Gear: Standard rack plus offwidth gear.

14. **El Gran Guano Blanco** [Geoff Parker, T.Taber, Jim Reston 1970s.] Unknown number of pitches. Starts left from *Dresdoom*. Pitch 1: Begin in shallow chimney with medium runout to spacious area. Pitch 2: Turn overhanging flake (block) to traverse. Left on face and up crack.

## C. WEST FORK OF OAK CREEK

Routes require hiking west up the West Fork Trail. Described north to south.

1. **The Equinox IV 5.9 A3+** [Mark Peterson, M. Lawson 1985.] Six pitches. 2.75 mi in on south side at giant roof/lightning bolt crack. Ends in chimney.
2. **Grapes of Wrath 5.10** [P. Davidson, Eileen Keller 1984.] Three pitches. Fifteen minutes up canyon to long north-to-south wall on south side. Follows northeast corner crack system.
3. **Eight Ball Tower - Rolling with the Eight Ball 5.9-** [Ray Vought, Greg Anderson 9/91.] Three pitches. Tower about 2 mi up West Fork on south side of stream. Pitch 1: Begin on east (downstream side) up easy but fugly chimney. Pitch 2: North face crack system. Pitch 3: Around west on ledge to bolt.

## D. COKE WALL AREA

Large 500' Coconino sandstone wall to west of Highway 89A, just south of mouth of West Fork of Oak Creek Canyon. Described north to south.

D. Coke Wall

1.  **Ophelia Bumps 5.10** [Bob Dubois, Jim Gaun 1988.] One pitch on low white face west from the Blair's house sign. Right of obvious right-facing corner north of Coke Wall.

2.  **Chameleon Corner 5.9 A1** [Dave Houchin, Ron Freitag 1984.] Three pitches. Left-facing corner system with pendulum.

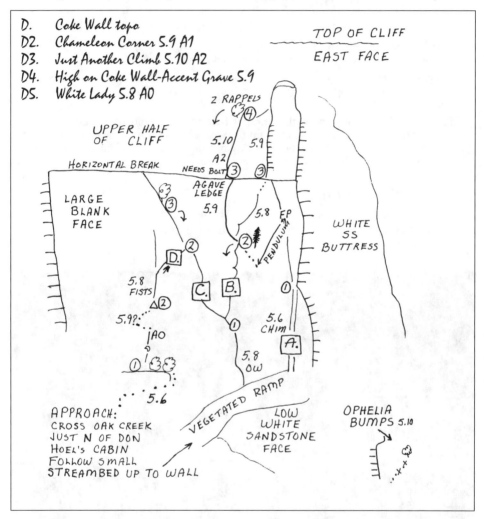

D.   *Coke Wall topo*
D2.  *Chameleon Corner 5.9 A1*
D3.  *Just Another Climb 5.10 A2*
D4.  *High on Coke Wall-Accent Grave 5.9*
D5.  *White Lady 5.8 A0*

3.  **Just Another Climb 5.10 A2** [D. Houchin, R. Freitag 1985.] Four pitches. Goes up off *High on Coke Wall-Accent Grave* after first pitch.

4.  **High on Coke Wall-Accent Grave 5.9** [Dugald Bremner, Bill Brent 1979.] Three to four itches. Right-facing hand and off-width dihedrals near right side of Coke Wall.

5.  **White Lady 5.8 A0** [D. Houchin, R. Freitag 1984.] Three pitches. South of *High on Coke Wall-Accent Grave.*

## E. SOUTH OF COKE WALL

This area includes routes south of the Coke Wall down to Encinoso Picnic Area west of Highway 89A. Described north to south.

1. **Sandcastle 5.10** [P. Davidson, J. Haisley early '80s.] Three pitches. Pyramidal Coconino sandstone wall above and to south of Slide Rock SP. North-face dihedrals left of center on Pitch 1: 5.9+ right-facing fingercrack. Pitch 2: 5.10 Off-width roof. Pitch 3: 5.8 sq chimney, descend to back.

2. **Counterfeit 5.7** [Brian Heydorn, Dave Keeber late '80s.] One pitch. One mile up Sterling Pass Trail on left. Righ-facing/arching corner system.

E1. Sandcastle Formation looming above Slide Rock State Park

## E1. OAK CREEK WATERFALL AREA

Park at Encinoso Picnic Area and walk north on Highway 89A 100 yards to parking pullout (alternate parking) on right. Basalt cliffs loom overhead to east. Ford stream via rocks (difficult in spring runoff?). Hike briskly up rock-lined drainage to waterfall (around 30 min). Routes are all one-pitch (<120') and described northwest to south. Protection is a standard rack with RPs and triples of some Friends on certain lengthy parallel cracks. Most routes have insitu rappels. Loose blocks are a hazard on some climbs for the first 30 feet.

Routes were first done here on the right side of the waterfall by John Gault, Steve Bartlett, Stan Mish, and T. Toula et al. Routes on the left side of the waterfall by Darren Singer, Tim Maloney, Jason Keith et al. Topo courtesy of Darren Singer. Superior routes are given a ★.

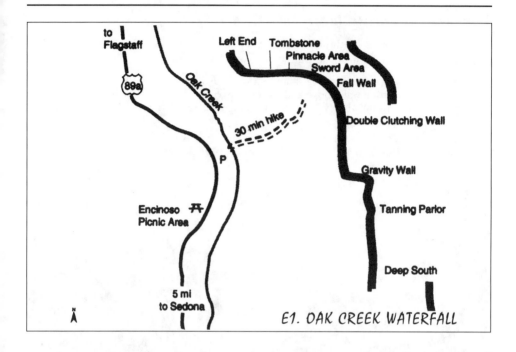

to
Flagstaff

89a

Oak Creek

30 min hike

P

Encinoso
Picnic Area

5 mi
to Sedona

Left End    Tombstone
Pinnacle Area
Sword Area
Fall Wall

Double Clutching Wall

Gravity Wall

Tanning Parlor

Deep South

E1. OAK CREEK WATERFALL

approach
gully

E1. Oak Creek Waterfall area
viewed from Encinoso Picnic Area

**Left End:** 50 yards left of *The Tyrant*, past broken area.
1. **Rising Sun 5.10-** ★ [Daniel Miller, Darren Singer, 1992.] Left double cracks.
2. **Original Sin 5.11 TR** [D. Singer, 1992.] Right side of areté.
3. **Ninja Warrior 5.10+** ★ [ D. Miller and D. Singer, 1992.] Right crack.

**Tombstone Area:** 100 yards left of waterfall.
4. **Dirty Deed 5.10** [D. Singer and Jason Keith, 1992.] Crack on left of headwall.
5. **The Tyrant 5.11+** ★ [D. Singer and D. Miller, 1992.] Middle crack of headwall. Variation start 5.11 TR.
6. **Noggin 'Nocker 5.10+** [D. Singer and J. Keith, 1992.] Crack on right of headwall. Loose.
7. **Tombstone 5.10** [D. Singer and D. Miller, 1992.] Loose start, good above.
8. **Mental Health 5.10** [Robert Warren, D. Singer and D. Miller, 1992.] Start right of flare.
9. **Outrageous 5.10+** [R. Warren, D. Singer and D. Miller, 1992.] Loose start, good above.
10. **Morticia 5.10+** ★ [D. Singer and D. Miller, 1992.] Thin.
11. **Uncle Fister 5.10** ★ [D. Miller and D. Singer, 1992.] Off-width.

**Pinnacle Area:** 80 yards left of waterfall.
12. **More Anus Than Heinous 5.10-** [J. Keith, 1992.] Off-width.
13. **Righteous Dump 5.10-** [J. Keith, 1992.] Small spring at base.
14. **Giardia Crack 5.11/5.11+** ★ [D. Miller and D. Singer, 1992.] Small spring at base.
15. **Nervous Breakdown 5.11** ★ [TR J. Keith, 1992, lead Singer, 1992.] Approach from 'C' or 'E.'
16. **Central Scrutinizer 5.11** ★ [D. Singer and D. Miller, 1992.]
17. **Spite and Malice 5.10+** ★ [D. Singer and D. Miller, 1992.] Classic overhanging hands.
18. **Insomnia 5.11** ★ [TR D. Singer and Miller 1992, lead Miller 1992.] Serious lead
19. **Terminator 5.12- TR** ★ [FA Keith, FFA 1992, TR Singer 1992.] Thin crack on face.
20. **Guacamole 5.11** ★ [D. Singer and D. Miller, 1992.] Stemming.
21. **Phlegm of Fury 5.11** [FA Warren, FFA (TR) 1992 Keith (lead) Singer 1992.] Deformed oak at start.
22. **Dihedral of Dagmar 5.10+** [D. Singer and D. Miller, 1992.] Hidden corner.
23. **Smoke Big Doobs, Suck Big Boobs 5.10+** ★ [Keith 1992.] Classic stem box.
24. **Thick and Thin 5.11** ★ [FA (TR) Miller 1992, (lead) Miller 1992.]
25. **Susie and Ishmael Do the Nasty 5.12** ★ **TR** [Miller 1993.] Arête.
26. **Flashflood 5.10-** ★ [Keith 1992.]
27. **Fool's Progress 5.11-** [Keith 1992.] Stemming in white corner.
28. **Earth Diver 5.11-** [Keith 1992.]

**Sword Area:** 40 yards left of waterfall.
29. **Nitrogenous Waste 5.11** [D. Singer and D. Miller, 1992.] Loose!
30. **Most Excellent 5.11** ★ [D. Singer and D. Miller, 1992.] Start out roof. Thin.

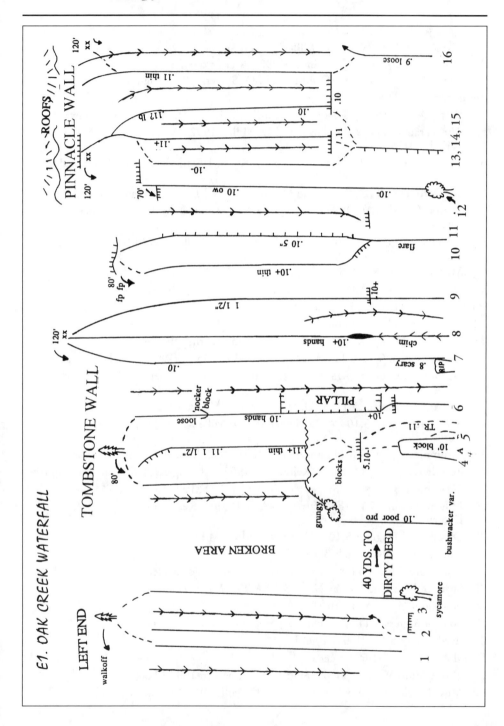

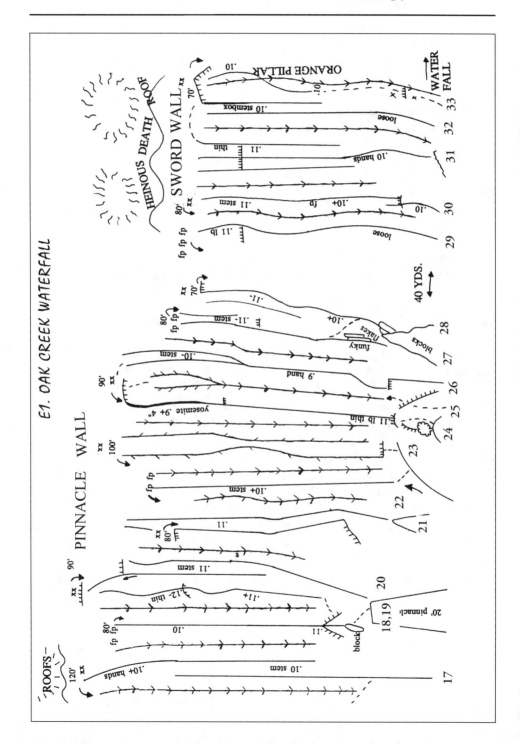

E1. OAK CREEK WATERFALL

31. **Vertebrae 5.11 TR** [Singer and Chris MacIntosh (lead) Singer 1992.] Through right side of roof. Belay on pillar.

32. **The Sword 5.10** ★ [D. Singer and D. Miller, 1992.] Left-side of pillar. Loose start.

33. **Bladerunner 5.10** ★ [TR D. Singer and D. Miller, 1992. Lead Singer and Miller 1992.] Areté to crack on pillar.

**Fall Wall:** Immediately right of waterfall.

34. **Black & Tan 5.10+** ★ {Singer and Jeff Huebner 1994.] Stem box through double roof.

35. **Lord Humongous 5.11-** ★ Obvious hand to fist crack.

36. **Lochs of Dread 5.12-?** ★ [D. Miller, 1992.] Thin hands to seam.

**Double Clutching Wall:** Between Fall Wall and where cliff rounds corner to left.

37. **No Feelings 5.10+** [Tim Toula, J. Gault 1981.] Face to double-hand crack capped by small block roof.

38. **5.11 TR** [D. Singer and D. Miller, 1992.]

39. **5.11-?** [D. Singer and D. Miller, 1992.] Obvious thin crack.

40. **Double Clutching 5.11-** ★ [T. Toula, Stan Mish 1985.] Crack follows two roofs out left.

**GRavity Wall:** 150 yards right of waterfall, where cliff shortens.

41. **The Chronic 5.12-?** ★ [Tim Maloney and Jon Govi 1993.] Thin corner through roof.

42. **Hands 5.10-** ★ [D. Singer 1993.] Short but good.

43. **Burning Bush 5.7** ★ TR [Jennifer Kearsley, (lead) Singer 1993.] Short but good.

44. **Tim's 5.11 5.11** ★ [Tim Maloney 1993.] Thin

**Tanning Parlor:** 200 yards right of waterfall in obvious alcove. All routes 50 feet high.

45. **Ozone 5.9** ★ TR [D. Singer, 1992. (lead) Singer 1992.] Wide.

46. **Yucca Valley Pants 5.11-** [Steve Bartlett and T. Toula 1983.]

47. **Eric's 5.10 5.10** ★ [Eric Mendt 1993.] Variation of B.

48. **Paba-Free 5.9** [D. Singer and E. Mendt, 1993.] Thin.

49. **UVA 5.10+** [D. Singer 1993.] Steep fists on top.

50. **Tube Socks & Chocks 5.8** ★ [T. Toula and S. Bartlett 1983.] Hands.

51. **Vertical Beaches 5.8** ★ [D. Singer 1993.]

52. **Fun in the Sun 5.6** ★ [D. Singer and J. Kearsley 1993.] Right-facing corner.

**Deep South**

53. **Appealing Nose 5.10c** ★ [S. Bartlett and T. Toula 1983.] Prominent crack through areté bulge.

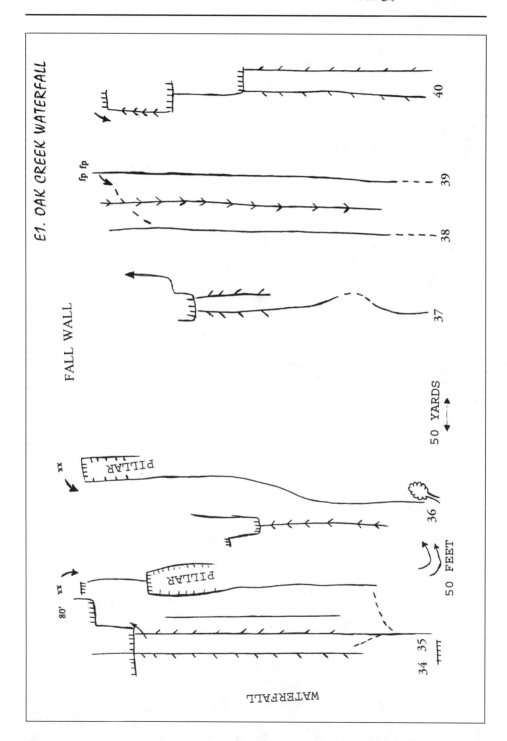

E1. OAK CREEK WATERFALL

FALL WALL

50 YARDS

50 FEET

WATERFALL

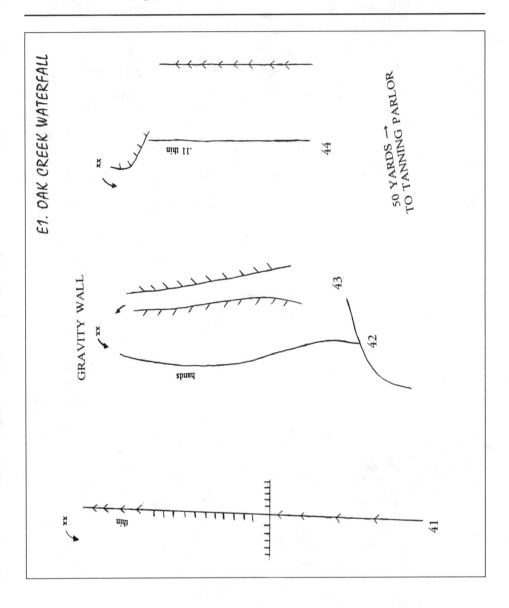

E1. OAK CREEK WATERFALL

50 YARDS → TO TANNING PARLOR

GRAVITY WALL

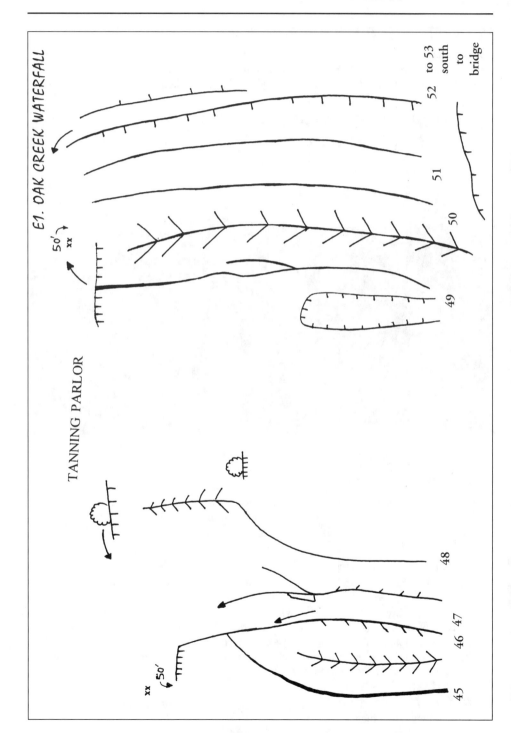

E1. OAK CREEK WATERFALL

TANNING PARLOR

50'

xx

45   46 47   48   49   50   51   52   to 53
                                              south
                                              to
                                              bridge

50'
xx

## E2. WEST OF ENCINOSO PICNIC AREA

Park at Encinoso Parking area and hike up Wilson Mountain Trail until bushwacking up right is feasible over red rock bench to Coconino sandstone wall. Routes established by Peter McFarlane, Mark Heimlich, Cameron Kern, Angelo Kokenakis in the early 1990s.

## E3. WILSON MOUNTAIN BASALTS (EAST BENCH)

Reports of routes being established here in the 1970s and into the '90s. Multipitched basalt climbs.

Wilson Canyon and Wilson Mtn from
Midgley Bridge Parking Area

## F. MIDGLEY BRIDGE AREA

Routes described east to west.)

Park at Midgley Bridge Parking Area for all these sandstone spire routes. Good toproping has been done on the rock bands below the bridge although the Forest Service has closed the area around the bridge to rock climbing for the same reason as Oak Creek Overlook Closure: visitor safety.

1. **Super Crack Tower 5.9** [T. Coats, Dave Dawson early '80s.] Three pitches. North lightning bolt cracks. Pitch 1 and 2: Up cracks. Pitch 3: Face. Bush rappell. Needs anchors.

2. **Lily Flower Tower 5.9** [Ross Hardwick, etal '70s.] Three pitches. Southwest Cracks 5.10 [E. Webster, L. Coats '70s.] Three pitches. Fist.

3. **Do Not Go Gentle Into That Good Fright 5.10+R/X** [T. Toula, Jim Symans, Kathy Zaiser 1987.] Two pitches. Handcrack on jutting buttress that appears as spire on NE/E bench below the Acropolis. Limestone ledge for walkoff back.

**(Steamboat) Submarine Rock**

4. [Unknown pre-1975.] Two pitches. Southeast side to northwest bolt ladder remnant. Bolt casings now plugged.

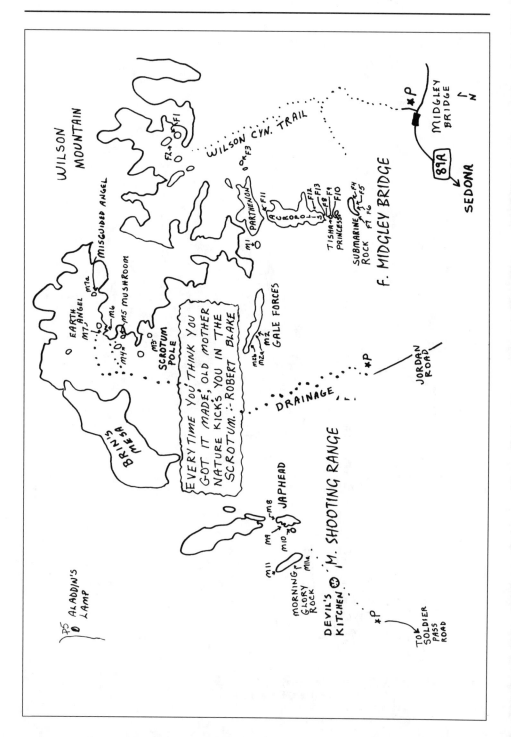

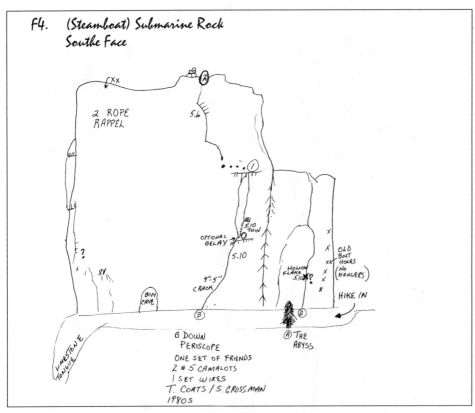

F4.   (Steamboat) Submarine Rock
      Southe Face

2 ROPE RAPPEL

5.6

5.10 THIN

OPTIONAL BELAY

5.10

4"-5" CRACK

BIVY CAVE

LIMESTONE TONGUE

?

OLD BOLT HOLES (NO HANGERS)

HOLLOW FLAKE 5.10+?

HIKE IN

B  DOWN PERISCOPE
ONE SET OF FRIENDS
2 # 5 CAMALOTS
1 SET WIRES
T. COATS / S. GROSSMAN
1980S

A  THE ABYSS

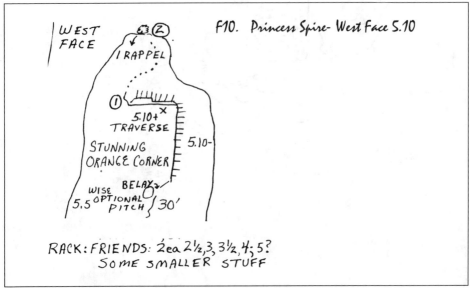

WEST FACE

1 RAPPEL

F10.   Princess Spire- West Face 5.10

5.10+ TRAVERSE

STUNNING ORANGE CORNER

5.10-

BELAY

WISE OPTIONAL PITCH  30'

5.5

RACK: FRIENDS: 2ea 2½, 3, 3½, 4; 5?
      SOME SMALLER STUFF

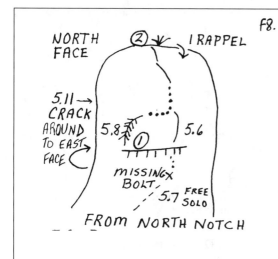

**F8.** Tisha Spire- Original N Face
Route 5.7

Rack: wires and 1 set of Friends

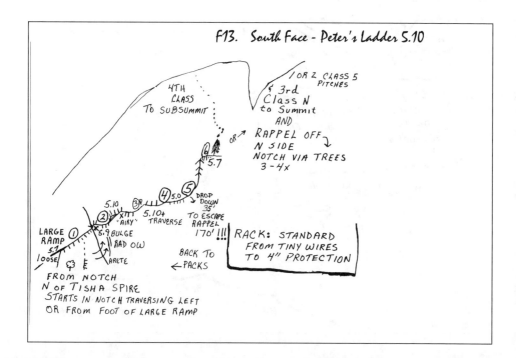

5. **The Abyss 5.10** [T. and L Coats 1980s.] Two pitches. Crack just left of Submarine to left-leaning diagonal system.

6. **Down Periscope 5.10** [T. Coats, S. Grossman '80s.] Two pitches. Middle south face. Pitch 1: Right-slanting ramp through dihedral face move. Pitch 2: Left up ramp. One rappel.

7. **Depth Charge 5.10** [S. Grossman, John Fleming '80s.] Two pitches. Crack on northwest side. Starts at base below limestone band.

**Tisha Spire**

8. **Original N Face Route 5.7** Two pitches. **Flake Var. 5.8** [S. Baxter etal 1978.] Two pitches.

9. **East Face Route** [L.Coats, Dugald Bremner 5.10 A1. FFA: 5.11 P. Davidson, S. Grossman 1978.] Two pitches. Crack. Good.

10. **Princess Spire- West Face 5.10+** [S. Baxter, Gordon Douglass early '80s.] One pitch. Left-facing orange dihedral and roof. Excellent classic.

**The Acropolis**

11. **North Face 5.7** [S. Baxter, Ross Hardwick, G. Douglass 1975.] Four pitches. Middle of north face. Start to a vegetated, dirty chimney.

12. **East Face 5.10** [S. Baxter, R. Hardwick 1978.] Four pitches. Left-leaning crack on left side of giant "ice cream cone."

13. **South Face - Peter's Ladder 5.10+** [T. and L.Coats, S. Baxter 1980s.] Five pitches. Across (north) from Tisha escape. 170' rappel or up to summit via 5.7/5.8 pitches and scrambling.

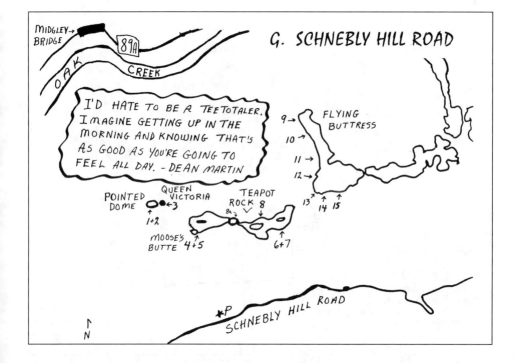

Pointed
Dome

Queen
Victoria

Moose's Butte

Thumbs Up

Teapot Rock

The Spout

The Pot

# G. SCHNEBLY HILL ROAD (NORTH OF THE ROAD)

These large, prominent sandstone formations are best reached via parking pullouts on Schnebly Hill Road. Hike north to formation of choice. Described from west to east.

1. **Pointed Dome-South Face 5.11-XX** [Bob Kamps, TM Herbert, Don Wilson 1959. FFA: R. Hardwick, S. Baxter, L. Coats, G. Douglass 1977.] Three pitches. South face. Right-facing corner to incredible and necky face(5.9 XX).

2. **Bolt Route?** [Pre-1977.] One pitch to right of 5.11- on last pitch. Memorial route to a climber's deceased father.

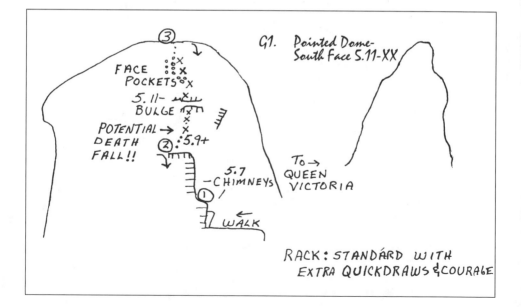

③
FACE
POCKETS
5.11-
BULGE
POTENTIAL →
DEATH
FALL!!
② :5.9+
5.7
-CHIMNEYS
①
WALK

G1. Pointed Dome-
South Face 5.11-XX

To →
QUEEN
VICTORIA

RACK: STANDARD WITH
EXTRA QUICKDRAWS & COURAGE

3. Queen Victoria 5.7 [Chuck Martens, date unknown.] Two to three pitches. East sky-
line route, loose.

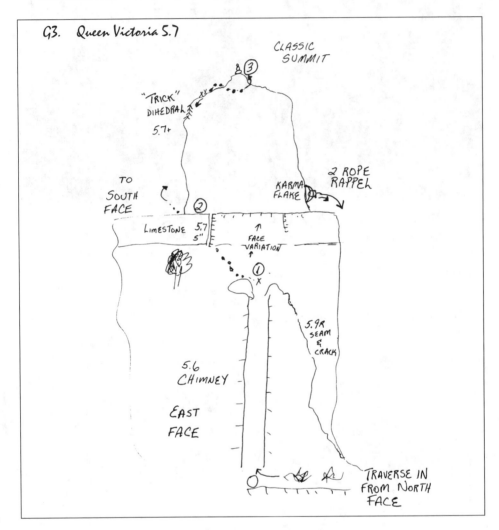

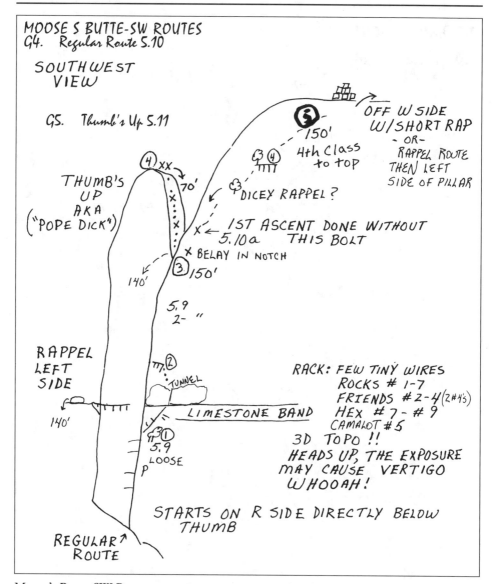

MOOSE S BUTTE-SW ROUTES
G4.  Regular Route 5.10

SOUTHWEST
   VIEW

G5.  Thumb's Up 5.11

THUMB'S
   UP
   AKA
("POPE DICK")

150'

OFF W SIDE
W/ SHORT RAP
- OR -
RAPPEL ROUTE
THEN LEFT
SIDE OF PILLAR

4th Class
to top

70'

DICEY RAPPEL ?

1ST ASCENT DONE WITHOUT
5.10a    THIS BOLT

BELAY IN NOTCH

140'

150'

5.9
2- "

RAPPEL
LEFT
SIDE

140'

TUNNEL

LIMESTONE BAND

5.9

LOOSE

RACK: FEW TINY WIRES
      ROCKS # 1-7
      FRIENDS # 2-4 (2#4's)
      HEX # 7 - # 9
      CAMALOT # 5
   3D TOPO !!
   HEADS UP, THE EXPOSURE
   MAY CAUSE VERTIGO
   WHOOAH!

STARTS ON R SIDE DIRECTLY BELOW
      THUMB

REGULAR
ROUTE

**Moose's Butte-SW Routes**

4. **Regular Route 5.10** [S. Baxter, R. Hardwick, Karl Karlstrom early '80s.] Four pitches. Summit bolt added on Pitch 3 after first ascent. Three rappels on left side.

5. **Thumb's Up 5.11** [Walt Shipley, Ira Hickman 1989.] Three pitches. Pitch 3 (5.11) cuts off Regular Route onto spire.

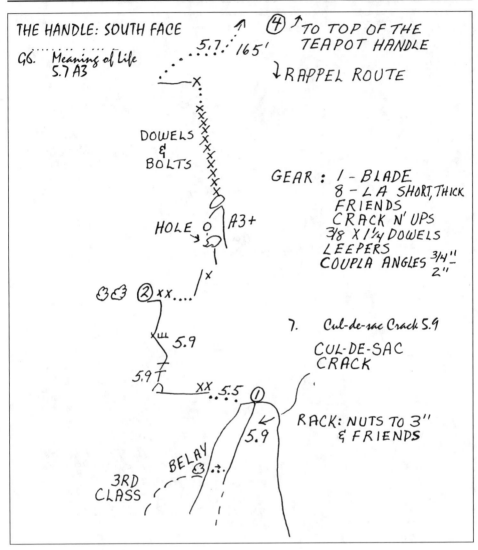

THE HANDLE: SOUTH FACE

G6. Meaning of Life
5.7 A3

5.7 165'

④ TO TOP OF THE
TEAPOT HANDLE

↓ RAPPEL ROUTE

DOWELS
&
BOLTS

HOLE A3+

GEAR : 1 - BLADE
8 - LA SHORT, THICK
FRIENDS
CRACK N' UPS
3/8 X 1 1/4 DOWELS
LEEPERS
COUPLA ANGLES 3/4"-2"

② xx....

5.9

5.9

XX 5.5 ①

5.9

7.   Cul-de-sac Crack 5.9

CUL-DE-SAC
CRACK

RACK: NUTS TO 3"
& FRIENDS

BELAY

3RD
CLASS

Teapot Rock
   The Handle: South Face
6.   Meaning of Life 5.7 A3+ [M. Lawson, Alex McGuffie 1983.] Four pitches. Starts at Cul-de-sac Crack.
7.   Cul-de-sac Crack 5.9 [M. Lawson, Jeff Ingels, Gene Harris 1981.] One pitch. The only obviously sweet handcrack on south face.
The Pot: North Face (5652 foot buttress)
8.   Tea for Two 5.9 [Brian Heydorn, Dave Keeber, Cap'n 1989.] Two pitches. Right-facing dihedral on left (east) side of north face.

## THE SPOUT

8a. There's a Matter of Your Dues 5.10+ A1 [Carl Tobin, John Middendorf, T. Toula 1993.] Four pitches. Pitch 1: Short north face, beak ladder. Pitch 2: Follow ridge to west, then up and right over 5.8 exposed step. Pitch 3: Follow 4th class ledge west to northwest side of tower. Pitch 4: 5.10+ crack to top.

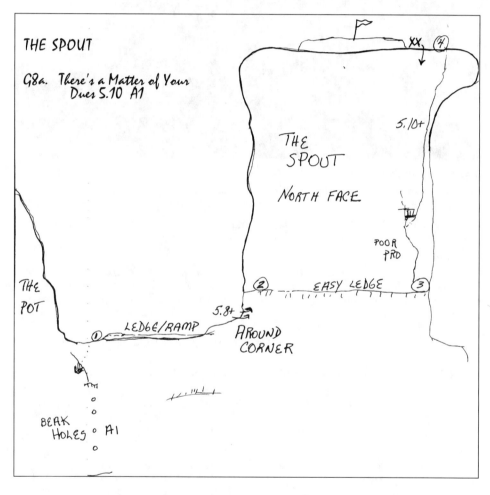

Area G

The Flying Buttress – North and Main West Face

## The Flying Buttress

From north to west to south. Rappel off north side.

### North Face

9.  **Original Northeast Ridge 5.8** [Dugald Bremner, Art Punt, R. Hardwick, L.Coats 1978.] Three pitches. Cracks to 4th class ridge to summit.

### West Face

10. **Epitaph** [M. Lawson, Glenn Rink(LB) 1984; FFA: M. Lawson, Pete Hill, A. McGuffie, John Rapp 1984.] Six pitches. Pitches 1 and 2: Right-facing dihedral. Pitch 3: Giant 50' roof traverse. Pitches 4 to 6: Unprotected traverses of 5.0, 5.8+, and straight up 5.7. Hike southeast to summit on ledge systems. Rappel off southwest down Technicolor Corner.

11. **Queen's Bishop 5.10** [Chris Dunn, LB, Tim Steffan, A. McGuffie 1982.] Four pitches.

12. **A-M Aidline IV A3?** [T. Applewhite, John Middendorf 1988.] Two pitches. Overhanging aid line.

13. **Coats-Peterson Route 5.8 A1** [T. and L.Coats, M. Peterson early '80s.] Two pitches plus 4th class. Main arête cracks at saddle. FFA: Pitch 1: It's a Breeze 5.11 [Dow Davis, T. Steffan 1989.] First pitch crack/dihedral.

### South Face: Flying Buttress continued

14. **Technicolor Corner 5.10** [M. Lawson, Bobbi Bensman, Chris Dunn 1983.] Three pitches. Large right-facing corner. Pitch 1: features a Crosley initial corner. Pitch 2: Quality corner crack. Pitch 3: Exciting finishing face pitch. Two double-rope rappels.

15. **Limestone Highway 5.10-R** [C. Dunn, G. Rink '80s.] Three pitches. 200'(?) right of Technicolor Corner. Fourth class 50' to right-facing corner. Pitches 1 and 2: Traverse west 250' on limestone band. Pitch 3: Up left-facing corner with fixed pro. One rappel. Unfinished.

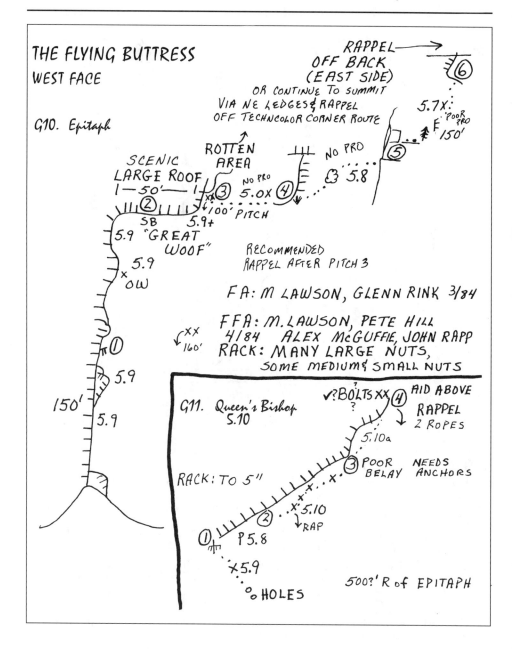

# THE FLYING BUTTRESS
## WEST FACE

G10. Epitaph

RAPPEL ⟶
OFF BACK
(EAST SIDE)
OR CONTINUE TO SUMMIT
VIA NE LEDGES & RAPPEL
OFF TECHNICOLOR CORNER ROUTE

⑥

5.7X
POOR
PRO
150'

ROTTEN
AREA

SCENIC
LARGE ROOF
1—50'—1

NO PRO
5.0X

⑤

NO PRO

③ 5.8

②

③

④

SB   5.9+
5.9 "GREAT
WOOF"

100' PITCH

5.9
x
OW

RECOMMENDED
RAPPEL AFTER PITCH 3

FA: M LAWSON, GLENN RINK 3/84

FFA: M. LAWSON, PETE HILL
4/84   ALEX McGUFFIE, JOHN RAPP
RACK: MANY LARGE NUTS,
SOME MEDIUM & SMALL NUTS

XX
160'

①

5.9

150'

5.9

G11. Queen's Bishop
5.10

?BOLTS XX ④
?

AID ABOVE
RAPPEL
2 ROPES

5.10a

③ POOR
BELAY

NEEDS
ANCHORS

RACK: TO 5"

② x 5.10
↓ RAP

① P 5.8

x 5.9

°° HOLES

500?' R of EPITAPH

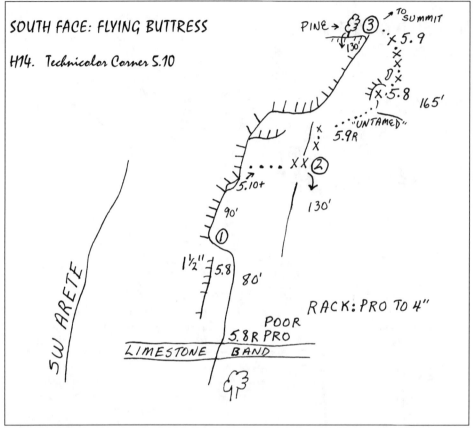

SOUTH FACE: FLYING BUTTRESS

H14. Technicolor Corner 5.10

PINE → ③ TO SUMMIT
× 5.9
×
×
×
×·5·8    165'
"UNTAMED"
× 5.9R
×
X X ②
5.10+    130'
90'
①
1½"⌐5.8    80'
POOR
5.8R PRO
LIMESTONE BAND
RACK: PRO TO 4"
SW ARETE

## H. SCHNEBLY HILL ROAD

South of road. These routes are located on first obvious Coconino sandstone buttress to south of Schnebly Hill Road. Described east to west.

**Temple of Diana (#1-9)**

1.  **Butterfly 5.10-** [Larry Bratten, Jay Anderson 1986.] Five pitches. Center crack of three perfect cracks. Starts offwith fists.

2.  **Temple of Diana 5.11** [P. Davidson, T. Coats 1980s.] Three pitches. Pitch 1: Obvious crack through three-tiered roofs to off-width. Pitch 2: 5.10 off-width. Pitch 3: 5.9 crack to top of buttress. Route lies left of center of this whole formation. Also known as Crazy Guggenheim.

3.  **Garden Party 5.7 A2** [Tom Cecil, Peterson 1986.] Four to five pitches. Aid start 30' left of The Black Pope Plays Cowboy.

4.  **The Sky 5.10+** [T. Cecil, Peterson 1986.] Two pitches. Left of two cracks high on wall, directly above The Black Pope. Escape via rappel or top out.

5.  **The Black Pope Plays Cowboy 5.10+** [Peterson, Brad Miller 1986.] One pitch. Right-facing dihedral at left side of big black wall(top of access gully).

6.  **Blind Faith 5.10+** [Henderson, T. Cecil 1986.] One pitch. Four bolts. 1000' west of The Black Pope.

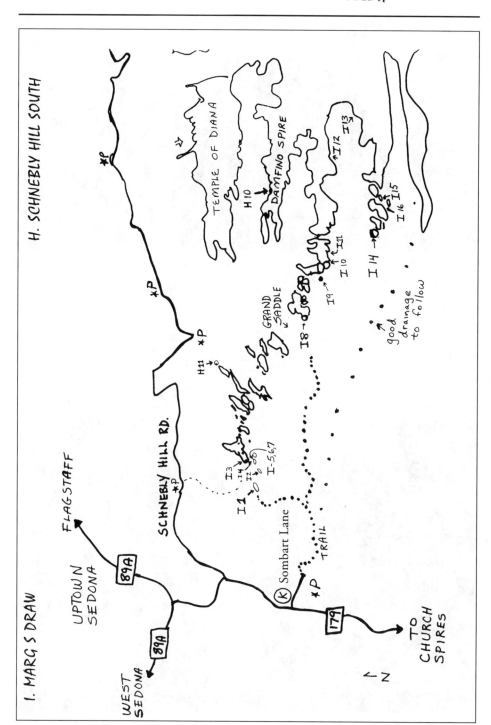

H. SCHNEBLY HILL SOUTH

I. MARG'S DRAW

*P

TEMPLE OF DIANA

H10

DAMFINO SPIRE

*P

GRAND SADDLE

I12

I13

I11

I10

I9

I8

I14

I15

I16

good drainage to follow

H11

*P

I3
I4
I2
I-5,6,7
I1
*P

SCHNEBLY HILL RD.

FLAGSTAFF

UPTOWN SEDONA

89A

WEST SEDONA

89A

Ⓚ Sombart Lane

*P TRAIL

179

TO CHURCH SPIRES

↙N

H. 1-9 Temple of Diana (North Face)

7. **Ripple 5.11** [T. Cecil, M. Miller, L. Henson 1986.] Crack in right-facing dihedral 600' east of The Black Pope.

8. **Shooting Star 5.10** [T. Cecil, Greg Knipe 1986.] One pitch. Crack to rappel above ledge. 10' right of Ripple.

9. **Deceptocrack 5.9** [Peterson, T. Cecil 1987.] One pitch. 7' right of and joins Shooting Star.

The following routes are accessed from first drainage on right, 1.9 mi up Schnebly Hill Rd.

Glen Rink on the giant dihedral of Damfino Spire

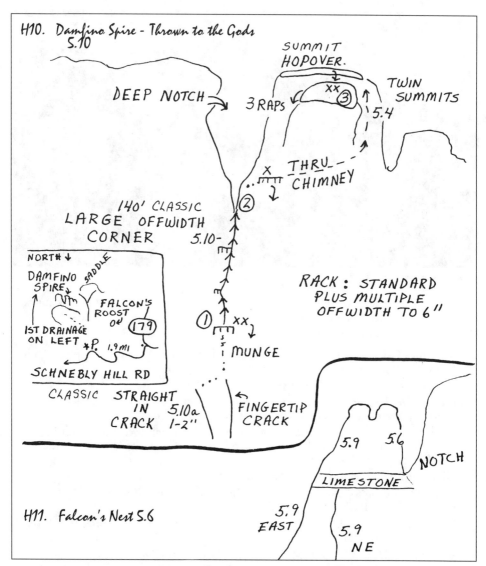

H10. Damfino Spire - Thrown to the Gods
5.10

SUMMIT
HOPOVER.

DEEP NOTCH

TWIN
SUMMITS

3 RAPS

XX
③

5.4

THRU
CHIMNEY

X

②

*140' CLASSIC*
LARGE OFFWIDTH
CORNER    5.10-

RACK: STANDARD
PLUS MULTIPLE
OFFWIDTH TO 6"

NORTH ↓
DAMFINO SPIRE ↘    SADDLE
FALCON'S
ROOST
ON ⑰⑨
1ST DRAINAGE
ON LEFT   *P. 1.9 mi
SCHNEBLY HILL RD

①  XX
MUNGE

CLASSIC STRAIGHT
IN   5.10a
CRACK   1-2"

FINGERTIP
CRACK

5.9   5.6

NOTCH

LIMESTONE

H11. Falcon's Nest 5.6

5.9
EAST

5.9
NE

10. **Damfino Spire - Thrown to the Gods 5.10+** [G. Rink, T. Toula 1986.] Four pitches. Large corner below visible large notch in Coconino Wall as seen from Schnebly Hill Road. One hour hike southeast up Damfino Canyon. Right-leaning fingercrack to large corner off-width to spire.

11. **Falcon's Nest 5.6** [S. Baxter, Sevak, Al Doty, T. Taber] One pitch from notch. 5.9 [S. Baxter, R. Hardwick 1989.] Two pitches. Cracks. First small spire on right, 1/4 mi up Damfino Canyon.

Camel's Head
Slingshot Rock
Tenacious Calculus
Grand Orcaface
King Crimson
I. Marg's Draw

# I. MARG'S DRAW

Just east of the Circle K at Sombart Lane, this large south-facing ridge of red rock spires leads east to the Coconino sandstone walls in the Munds Mountain Wilderness. Described west to east. See overview map pag 57.

1. **Tenacious Calculus 5.10+/11-** [D. Davis, S. Mish, T. Toula 1986.] One pitch. Spire (cluster) west and below Snoopy,. Good north face crack.

2. **Snoopy Nose Route 5.8** [First ascent unknown.]

3. **Camel's Head-Hand of Sceiron 5.10 A1** [Scott Martin, Bruce Edwards, RT 1987.] Three pitches. Crack system on northwest side of formation.

4. **Frosted Flakes 5.10** [Dave Insley, S. Mish, etal 1987. Final three pitches finished to top by Tim Kudo, Glen Rink 1992.] Five pitches. Face opposite Slingshot Rock Notch.

5. **Slingshot Rock-** Twinned spires that form a slingshot.

   **East Tower- Orig 5.7 A1** [Geoff Parker, Tom Taber 1970s.] Three pitches. North face from notch. Pitch 2 has bolt ladder.

6. **Free variation** [T. Toula, K. Zaiser 1989.] Pitch 2: 5.10+ Crack. Pitch 3: B1 TR on top left side of west face block.

7. **West Tower South Face 5.9** [M. Peterson, J. Ingels '80s.] Three pitches. Pitch 1: Same as *Tenacious Calculus* to notch. Pitch 2: Traverse southeast to Pitch 3: South cracks. Pitch 4: Summit crack.

8. **Grand Orcaface 5.8 A2** [G. Parker, T. Taber 1970s.] Two pitches. From nourtheast north to bolt holes.

9. **Firecat Spire 5.9** [G. Parker, etal. FFA: R. Hardwick, K. Karlstrom. Kim Spence direct 5.10 start 1970s.] Three pitches. From notch Pitch 1: traverse. Pitch 2: finger-crack to off-width. Pitch 3: Hueco off-width to left crack (right crack, 5.11). Pitch 4: face to top.

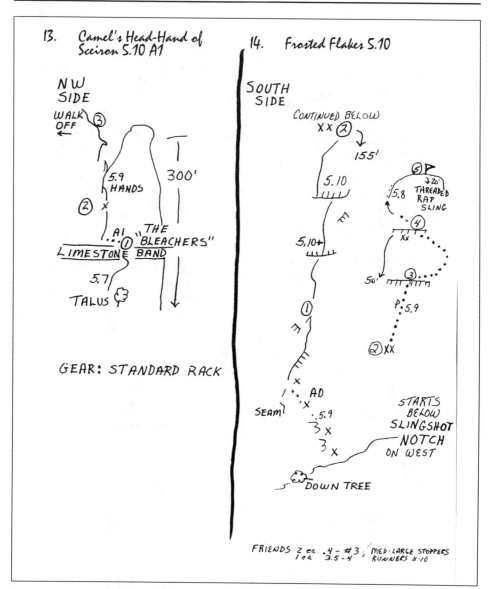

13. *Camel's Head-Hand of Sceiron* 5.10 A1

NW SIDE

WALK OFF ←  ③

5.9 HANDS

300'

② X

A1  "THE BLEACHERS"

LIMESTONE BAND ①

5.7

TALUS

GEAR: STANDARD RACK

14. *Frosted Flakes* 5.10

SOUTH SIDE

CONTINUED BELOW
X X ②

155'

5.10

5.10+

①

SEAM
A0
X
.5.9
3 X
3 X

DOWN TREE

⑤ P
↓20'
5.8  THREADED RAP SLING

④
XX

50'  ③
P.5.9

②XX

STARTS BELOW SLINGSHOT NOTCH ON WEST

FRIENDS 2 ea. .4 - #3 ; MED·LARGE STOPPERS
1 ea  3.5 - 4   RUNNERS 8·10

(?) **Lower Tower 5.9R** [L. Coats, E. Webster.] 5.11-TR of left-facing off-width dihedral at starting traverse T. Toula 1994; ("viva la bong sandwich")

10. **Screaming Besingi 5.8** [G. Parker, Lee Dexter 1973.] Two pitches. Pitch 1: Fantastic east chimney. Pitch 2: Poorly protected south face hump to summit. One double-rope rappel.

11. **Gunshy 5.11+/12-** [Richard Cilley, T. Toula 1987.] One pitch. 35' corner to roof crack on main wall east of Firecat Spire. Fixed nut rappel. Off-width crack above unclimbed.

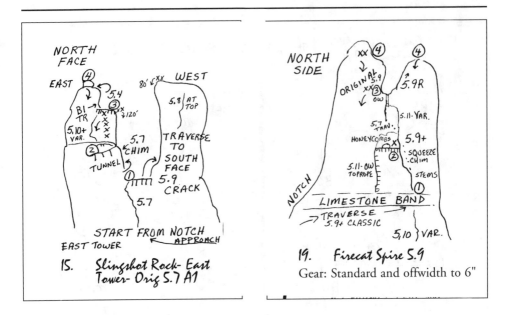

NORTH FACE

EAST ④

5.4
BI TR
5.10+ VAR.
②
TUNNEL
①
TUNNEL
5.7 CHIM

80' xx WEST
5.8 AT TOP
③ ↕120'

TRAVERSE TO SOUTH FACE 5.9 CRACK

5.7

START FROM NOTCH
EAST TOWER ← APPROACH

15. Slingshot Rock - East Tower - Orig 5.7 A1

NORTH SIDE

NOTCH

xx ④
ORIGINAL 5.9
xx ③ OW
5.7 TRAV.
HONEYCOMBS
②
5.11 OW TOPROPE

④
5.9 R
5.11 VAR.
5.9+ SQUEEZE CHIM
STEMS
①

LIMESTONE BAND
→ TRAVERSE →
5.9+ CLASSIC

5.10 } VAR.

19. Firecat Spire 5.9
Gear: Standard and offwidth to 6"

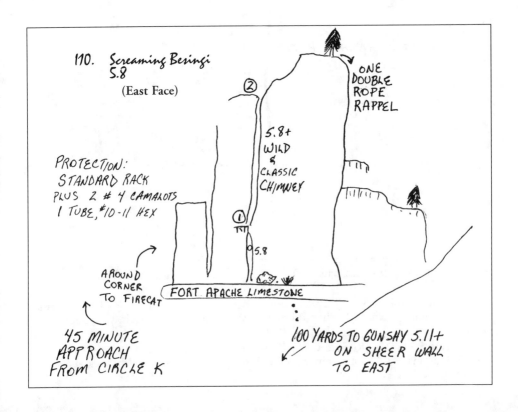

110. Screaming Besingi 5.8
(East Face)

②

ONE DOUBLE ROPE RAPPEL

5.8+ WILD & CLASSIC CHIMNEY

PROTECTION: STANDARD RACK PLUS 2 # 4 CAMALOTS 1 TUBE, #10-11 HEX

①
5.8

FORT APACHE LIMESTONE

AROUND CORNER TO FIRECAT

45 MINUTE APPROACH FROM CIRCLE K

100 YARDS TO GUNSHY 5.11+ ON SHEER WALL TO EAST

Richard Cilley loading up on Gunshy

12. **Blood, Sweat, and Fears 5.8** [P. Davidson, T. Coats 1980s.] One pitch. Red flat corner to chimney way east of *Screaming Besingi* and *Gunshy*. Sorry for nondescript directions.

13. **Jumping Jack Thrash 5.10 A2** [R. Hardwick, Davidson, Coats l980s.] Four pitches. Wall/corner on Coconino sandstone. Long wide crack system. Most obvious route, "way back there."

14. **King Crimson A3+** [S. Grossman, P. Davidson, T. and L. Coats '80s.] Two pitches. Beautiful right-facing corner system on west face of spire.

15. **Maceta 5.9 A1** [T. and L.Coats, J. Haisley, K. Karlstrom 1980s.] Three pitches. South hands/fists.

16. **Fire Hydrant Spire 5.10** [Dave Dawson, T. Coats 1980s.] Two pitches. North face-handcrack. Good.

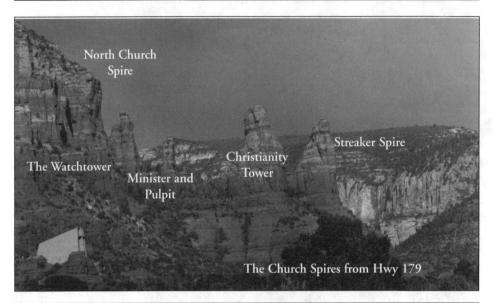

*The Church Spires from Hwy 179*

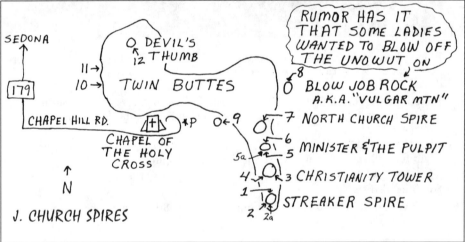

# J. THE CHURCH SPIRES

This classic cluster of spires lies just east of The Chapel of the Holy Cross. Devil's Thumb is north of the chapel. Described south to northwest.

### Streaker Spire

1. **Original Route 5.7** [S. Baxter, K. Karlstrom, R. Hardwick, G. Parker 1972.] Three pitches. From north north. Pitch 1: traverse limestone band to west face. Pitches 2 and 3: Up cracks.

2. **Southwest Corner Route** [Ascent?]

2a. **Re-animator Route 5.10 A2** [Barry Ward, Alan Humphrey] Starts at center of south face.

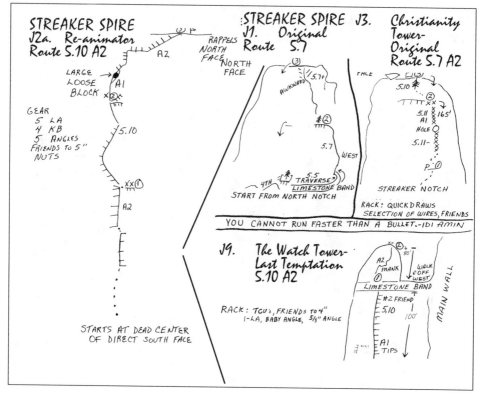

Christianity Tower-(Beckey's Spire)

3. Southeast Face Original Route 5.7 A2 [Fred Beckey 1970? 5.11 A0 T. Toula, Pete McFarlane 1986.] Three pitches. Six feet of aid remain on bolt ladder.

4. West Face-Isaac's Route  aka A Blast From the Past  5.9 [Tom Isaacs, LB, Jeff Bowman 1980s.] Five pitches. Classic face to handcrack on Pitch 1. Rappel Beckey Route.

5. Minister and the Pulpit- Kamps Route 5.7 [B. Kamps 1950s.] Two pitches from south notch. Pitch 1: Corner past block. Pitch 2: Up chim to crack.

5a. Phillips Route 5.9+R/X [Courtney Phillips, Wesley James 1994.] Left side of pendant to splitter crack. Rappel the route. Very poor pro at start.

6. North Face- 5.8 [S. Baxter etal.]

7. North Church Spire-5.7 [R. Hardwick, Paul Gleason 1975.] Two to three pitches. North notch to chimney to west notch to south chimney.

8. Blow Job Rock-Northeast Face 5.8 [G. Parker, T. Taber 1970s.] Two to three pitches. Northside recess twin cracks to notch to southside chimney. Good.

9. The Watch Tower- Last Temptation 5.10 A2 [C. Dunn, Jim Erdman 1989.] Two pitches. East face. Pitch 1: Bee-oo-tiful finger crack/corner. Pitch 2: Chossy aid.

10. Altar Boys Walk the Plank 5.10+ [Chris Goplerud, RT 1987.] One pitch. On low wall to north of Chapel Road at first bend from Highway 179. 35' right-leaning finger to handcrack in arched alcove. Tops out at roof with pins.

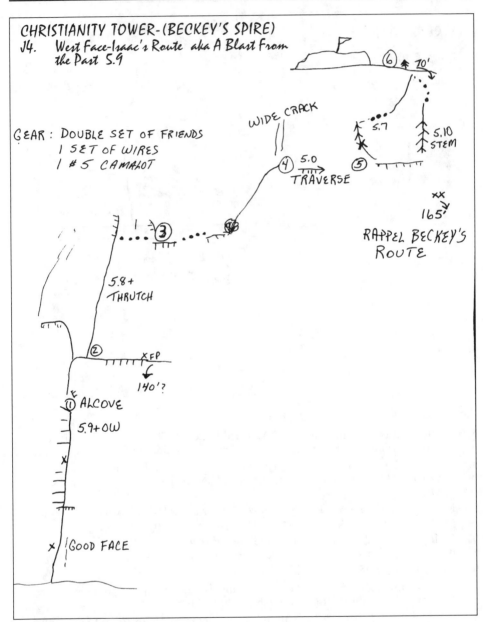

CHRISTIANITY TOWER-(BECKEY'S SPIRE)
J4.   West Face-Isaac's Route aka A Blast From the Past 5.9

GEAR :  DOUBLE SET OF FRIENDS
        1 SET OF WIRES
        1 # 5 CAMALOT

WIDE CRACK

④  5.0  → TRAVERSE

⑤

⑥  ↑ 70'

5.7

5.10 STEM

xx
165'
RAPPEL BECKEY'S ROUTE

③

5.8+ THRUTCH

②  X FP
   ↓
   140'?

① ALCOVE

5.9+OW

X

X  GOOD FACE

11. **Chapel Ruin 5.9** [R. Thorne, Scott Martin 1986.] Two pitches. 60' north of Altar Boys. Large right-facing corner to tree rappel.

12. **Devil's Thumb (Lost Chapel Spire) Bearded Clam Route 5.7** [T. Taber, Scott Sellers, and Bill Hickock '70s.] One pitch. Southeast chimney. Spire on NW side of Twin Buttes.

Courthouse Butte
(NW Corner)

Bell Rock (N Face)

# K. BELL ROCK AREA

This area covers formations from Bell Rock east to Jacks Canyon. Described west to east.

1. **Bell Rock 5.8** [B. Kamps etal.] One pitch. Fourth class us west gully to limestone band. Traverse southeast to north cracks. Several route variations have been done to summit

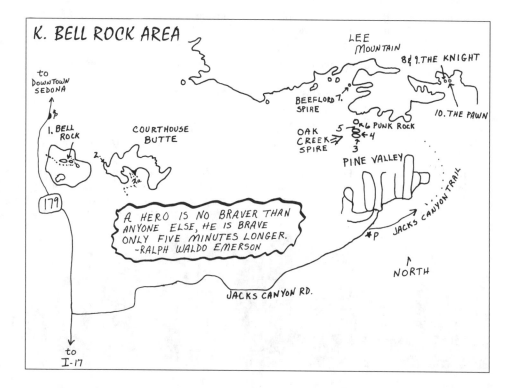

## K. BELL ROCK AREA

LEE
MOUNTAIN

8 & 9. THE KNIGHT

to
DOWNTOWN
SEDONA

BEEFLORD 7.
SPIRE

10. THE PAWN

1. BELL
ROCK

COURTHOUSE
BUTTE

OAK
CREEK
SPIRE

ORG PUNK ROCK

5
6
4
3

2.

2a

179

PINE VALLEY

JACKS CANYON TRAIL

A HERO IS NO BRAVER THAN
ANYONE ELSE, HE IS BRAVE
ONLY FIVE MINUTES LONGER.
-RALPH WALDO EMERSON

P  JACKS CANYON TRAIL

NORTH

JACKS CANYON RD.

to
I-17

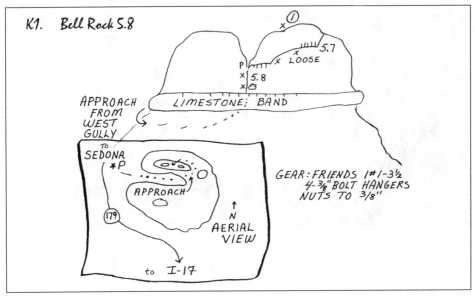

K1. Bell Rock 5.8

APPROACH FROM WEST GULLY

LIMESTONE; BAND

5.7 LOOSE

5.8

TO SEDONA

APPROACH

N AERIAL VIEW

GEAR: FRIENDS 1#1-3½ 4-⅜" BOLT HANGERS NUTS TO ⅜"

to I-17

2. **Courthouse Butte-A Day in Court 5.11+** [W. Shipley, K. Zaiser 1989.] Five pitches. Left-facing corner 200' right of largest left-facing corner on northwest buttress. Sustained and difficult. Ooo-ah…

2a. **Central South Rib 5.6** Hike to south bowl and south central rib. Begin technical rock climbing in tree for 2 pitches. Hike to summit. Spectacular views.

2b. **North Face Route 5.?** Described in summit register as ghastly.

3. **Oak Creek Spire-South Face** [M. Lawson et al.] Two ptiches. Right-facing dihedrals. Unfinished to top.

4. **Original East Chimney 5.9** [Bob Kamps, TM Herbert, Don Wilson 1970s.] Four pitches.

5. **North Face-West Crack 5.9-** [Ed Webster, etal 1970s.] Four pitches.

6. **Punk Rock-Devo Dihedral 5.9R** [T. and L.Coats, P. Davidson, J. Haisley 1980s.] Two pitches. Southeast face.

7. **Beeflord Spire-Pump First Then Pay 5.11+X A0 (5.12-TR)** [K. Zaiser, T. Toula, Ira Hickman 1989.] Two pitches. Totem Pole-like needle northwest of Oak Creek Spire. B.A.T. "bad acid trip" from east notch. Another ooo-ah route.

Oak Creek Spire

Punk Rock

The Knight, The Pawn

K. Lee Mountain South Face

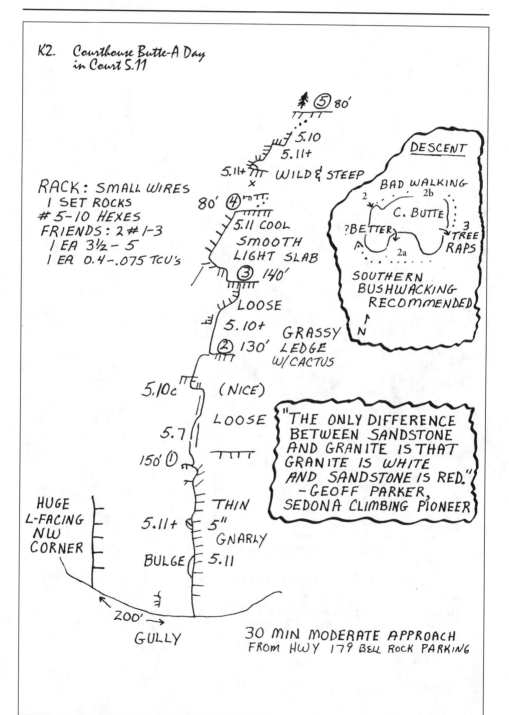

K2. Courthouse Butte-A Day
in Court 5.11

⑤ 80'

5.10
5.11+

5.11+  WILD & STEEP

RACK: SMALL WIRES
 1 SET ROCKS
 # 5-10 HEXES
 FRIENDS: 2 # 1-3
 1 EA 3½ - 5
 1 EA 0.4-.075 TCU's

80' ④

5.11 COOL
SMOOTH
LIGHT SLAB

③ 140'

LOOSE

5.10+      GRASSY
② 130'     LEDGE
           W/CACTUS

5.10c    (NICE)

LOOSE

5.7

150' ①

THIN

HUGE
L-FACING
NW
CORNER

5.11+   5"
        GNARLY
BULGE   5.11

200'

GULLY

**DESCENT**

BAD WALKING
2              2b
    C. BUTTE
?BETTER              3
A                   TREE
        2a          RAPS

SOUTHERN
BUSHWACKING
RECOMMENDED

↑
N

"THE ONLY DIFFERENCE
BETWEEN SANDSTONE
AND GRANITE IS THAT
GRANITE IS WHITE
AND SANDSTONE IS RED."
— GEOFF PARKER,
SEDONA CLIMBING PIONEER

30 MIN MODERATE APPROACH
FROM HWY 179 BELL ROCK PARKING

## Area K

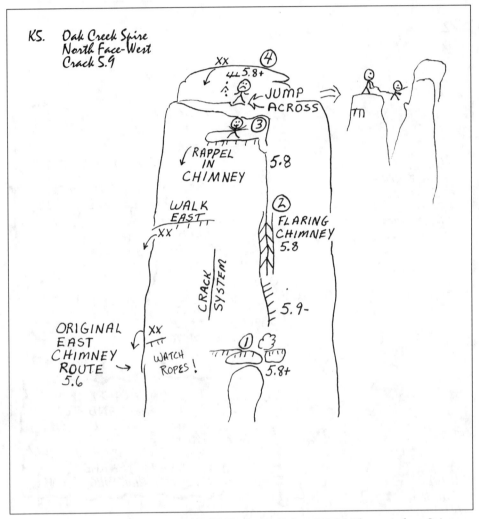

K5. Oak Creek Spire
North Face-West
Crack 5.9

XX
5.8+
④
JUMP
ACROSS
③
RAPPEL
IN
CHIMNEY
5.8
WALK
EAST
XX
②
FLARING
CHIMNEY
5.8
CRACK SYSTEM
5.9-
ORIGINAL
EAST
CHIMNEY
ROUTE
5.6
XX
WATCH
ROPES!
①
5.8+

8. **The Knight-Southeast Face 5.9R** [T. Toula, K. Zaiser 1989.] Three pitches. Spire to east summit.

9. **Checkmate 5.10R** [T. Toula, K. Zaiser 1989.] Three pitches. North face traverse to upper arête.

10. **The Pawn- On Golden Pawn 5.11-R/X A0** [T. Toula, K. Zaiser 1989.] Three pitches. Spire south face. Just east of Checkmate.

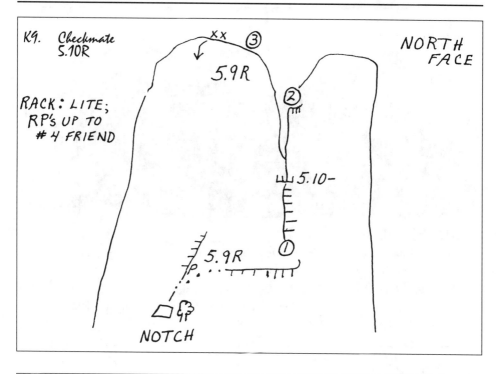

K9.  Checkmate
5.10R

xx  ③

5.9R

RACK: LITE;
RP's UP TO
  #4 FRIEND

②

5.10-

①

5.9R
P.

NORTH
FACE

NOTCH

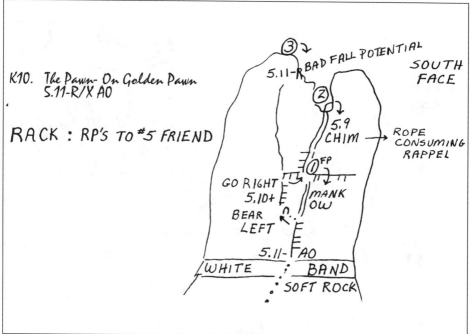

K10.  The Pawn- On Golden Pawn
5.11-R/X AO

RACK: RP's TO #5 FRIEND

③  BAD FALL POTENTIAL
5.11-R

②

5.9
CHIM

FP  ①

GO RIGHT
5.10+

BEAR
LEFT

MANK
OW

5.11- AO

WHITE  BAND

SOFT ROCK

SOUTH
FACE

ROPE
CONSUMING
RAPPEL

Cathedral Rock from Back-O-Beyond Rd.

The Mace — Middle Mesa — North Mesa — NW Pinnacle

## L. CATHEDRAL SPIRES

"Courthouse Butte" say the oldtimers. Described south to north. This area includes all the towers incorporated into the Cathedral Spires.

1. **South East Mesa Buttress Fourth Class** from south side.
2. **South Mesa- Rescue Route** [Sedona Fire Dept. Rescue 1987.] One pitch. Handcrack to three-bolt rappel. Site of only accident to date.

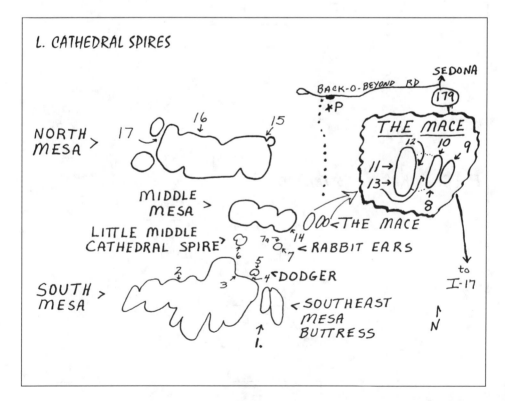

3. **Coats-Grossman Route 5.10+** [1980s.] Two pitches. Groove west of South Mesa-Rescue Route's notch.

3a. **200,000 Light Years From Home 5.7 A2** [Ray Vought (solo) 1992.] One pitch. 130' mixed aid/free.

**South Mesa Pinnacle**: Directly south of Rabbit Ears.

4. **The Dodger 5.9** [R. Hardwick, G. Parker, P. Gleason 1972.] Two pitches. Crack in notch south of #13. Crack to off-width ledge. "Room" to large chimney. Bring off-width gear.

5. **Bolt Ladder?** Face/off-width crack system on north face, faces Rabbit Ears. Bolts on ladder missing at start.

6. **Little Middle Cathedral Spire 5.9X** [G. Parker, S. Baxter, R. Hardwick, T. Taber 1970s.] Two pitches. South face desperate.

7. **Rabbit Ears East Face 5.7?** One pitch. South face of pinnacle south of Mace (near Medicine Wheel).

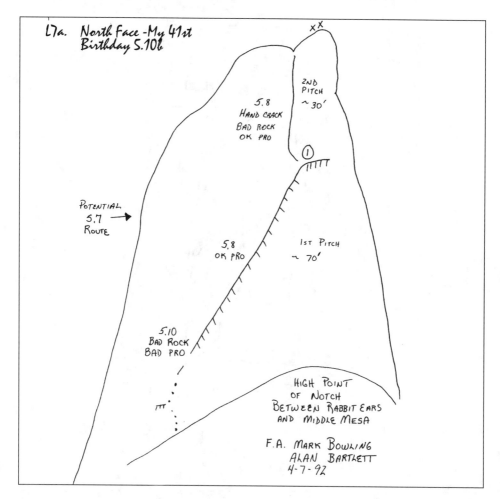

7a. North Face -My 41st Birthday 5.10b [Mark Bowling, Alan Bartlett 4/92.] Pitch 1: Distinct right-leaning ramp. Pitch 2: Short handcrack.

8. The Mace-Carson Memorial 5.10- Traverse limestone band south to crack system,rejoins Webster's Route.

9. Webster's Route 5.10 [Ed Webster, etal 1970s.] East side. Rejoins Webster's Route.

10. Original Route 5.9+ [Bob Kamps, TM Herbert, Dave Rearick 1957.] Five pitches. Pitch 1: Wide crack up to limestone. Pitch 2: Limestone roof to off-width to ledge. Pitch 3: Step across then up chimney. Pitch 4: hand to off-width crack. Pitch 5: Step across face mantle 5.9+ or right to flake 5.8, optional "jump back" across. A must do, most often climbed spire in Sedona.

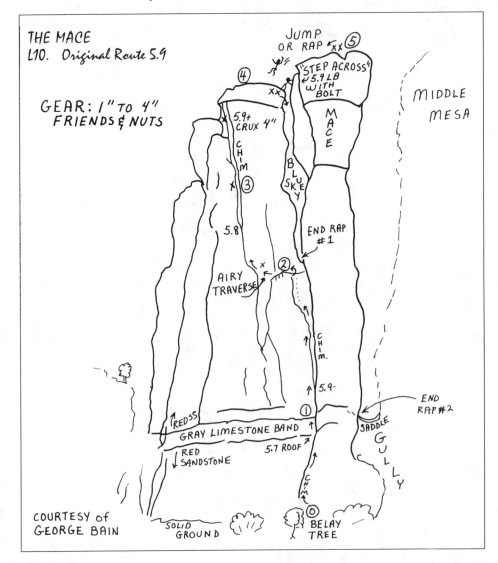

THE MACE
L10. Original Route 5.9

GEAR: 1" TO 4" FRIENDS & NUTS

COURTESY of GEORGE BAIN

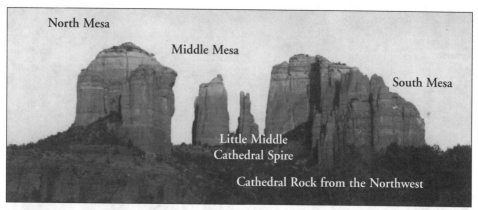

North Mesa

Middle Mesa

South Mesa

Little Middle
Cathedral Spire

Cathedral Rock from the Northwest

11. **Wind, Sand, and Stars 5.11** [T. and L.Coats, B. Bensman 1980s.] Pitch 1: In notch left of Blood, Sweat, and Tears. Traverse south to Pitch 2.

12. **Blood, Sweat, and Tears 5.10+** [T. Coats, B. Bensman 1980s.] Pitch 2 of Wind, Sand and Stars upper east facecrack of tallest spire.

13. **Rappel Route 5.10** [S. Baxter, R. Hardwick, G. Douglass late '70s.] Two pitches. Starts in notch up right cracks to inside west crack of middle spire.

14. **Middle Mesa-N Face-(Tough Crack to Nut) 5.9** [S. Baxter, R. Thompson 1977.] Two pitches. Hands to long chimney on east face across from Mace Rappel.

15. **North Mesa -NE Buttress- The Dong 5.10 A1 (5.11TR)** [L. and T. Coats, P. Davidson, S. Grossman 1980s.] Three pitches. Right-facing corner to face.

16. **N Face Pinnacle (aka Jailhouse Rock) 5?** [G. Parker and P.E. Major 1970.] One pitch. Old machine nut and sling to bolted rappel, lieback to jam bulge.

17. **NW Pinnacle-W. Chimney 5.?**

Pete McFarlane on the limestone traverse of Streaker Spire

The Mushroom

Jap Head

Morning Glory
Spire

M. Behind the Shooting Range

## M. BEHIND THE SHOOTING RANGE (JORDAN ROAD)

A large area of spires and fins west of the Acropolis and on both sides of Mormon Canyon. Described east to west. (See Section F aerial map, page ***.)

1.  **Ripoff Rock 5.6** [Tim Coats, etal 1980s.] One pitch. Spire northwest of Acropolis. Mostly 4th class from backside—proving once again that looks can be deceiving.

**Southwest Face 5667' Butte**

2.  **Gale Forces 5.9** [Tim Coats, etal 1980s.] Four pitches. Right-facing dihedral on south face of 5667' Buttress. Groddy.

2a. **The Fin 5.7** [Ray Vought, Sue Alpern]

2b. **The Tonya Harding Club 5.10** [Dave Bloom, Michael Hren] Aid seam to summit. Route unfinished.

3.  **Scrotum Pole 5.10R** [E. Webster, Bryan Becker] Two to three pitches. From notch, traverse west past 2 bolts to crack. Appropriately named tower.

4.  **Goliath 5.9** [S. Baxter, G. Douglass 1970s.] Three pitches. Spire from notch. North of Mushroom Gully with prominent boulder atop summit.

5.  **The Mushroom 5.10 A2** [J. Middendorf, S. Mish 1987.] Six pitches. Spire from northwest gully. Classic face pitch leads to exposed bolt ladder.

6.  **Looking For An Angel 5.11 A1** [T. Toula, K. Zaiser 1989.] Two to three pitches. Pitch 1: Off-width to ledge, traverse west. Pitch 2: Left-facing corner. Pitch 3: Obvious splitter facecrack to fixed stopper (5.11+/5.12-). Unfinished aid past stopper. Southwest of Earth Angel.

7.  **Earth Angel 5.10** [S. Baxter, R. Hardwick 1975. Two-pitch traverse variation, Angel of Mercy, from Pitch 7 5.10+R/X J. Gault, T. Toula 1981.] Nine pitches. Begins on west side ledge. Sedona's longest spire route (see topo).

7a. **Misguided Angel 5.7 A2** [Ray Vought 1992.] One pitch. Small tower with unique angular appearance east (upcanyon) and on same side of canyon from Earth Angel. Crux is the approach.

M. BEHIND THE SHOOTING RANGE (JORDAN ROAD)
2.    Gale Force S.9
2a.   The Fin S.7
2b.   The Tonya Harding Club S.10

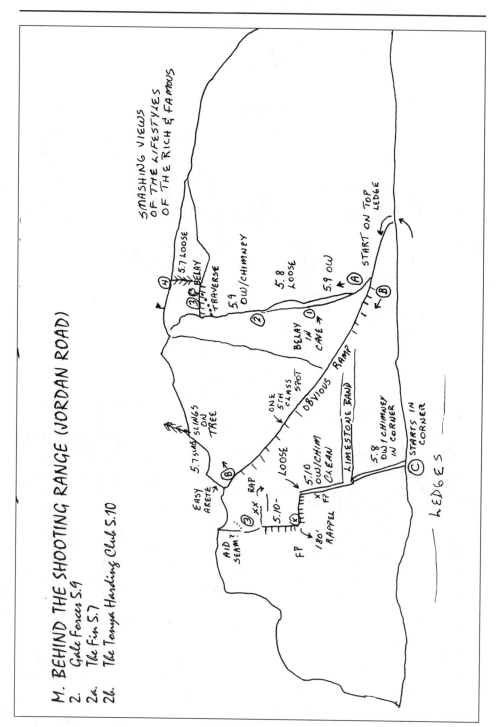

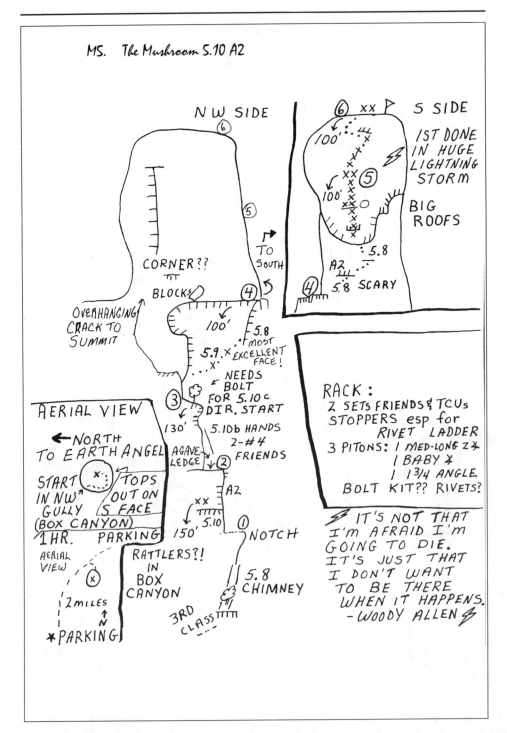

M5. The Mushroom 5.10 A2

NW SIDE

S SIDE

⑥ xx

1ST DONE IN HUGE LIGHTNING STORM

100'

100'

⑤

BIG ROOFS

TO SOUTH

CORNER??

BLOCKS

5.8

A2    5.8 SCARY

④

④

OVERHANGING CRACK TO SUMMIT

100'

5.8 MOST EXCELLENT FACE!

5.9. X
X

③

NEEDS BOLT FOR 5.10c DIR. START

AERIAL VIEW

130'

5.10b HANDS 2-#4 FRIENDS

NORTH

TO EARTH ANGEL

AGAVE LEDGE

②

A2

START IN NW GULLY (BOX CANYON)

TOPS OUT ON S FACE

RACK:
2 SETS FRIENDS & TCUs
STOPPERS esp for
    RIVET LADDER
3 PITONS: 1 MED-LONG Z
          1 BABY
          1 1 3/4 ANGLE.
BOLT KIT?? RIVETS?

1 HR.    PARKING

xx
5.10

150'

①

NOTCH

AERIAL VIEW

RATTLERS?!
IN
BOX
CANYON

5.8 CHIMNEY

⚡ IT'S NOT THAT I'M AFRAID I'M GOING TO DIE. IT'S JUST THAT I DON'T WANT TO BE THERE WHEN IT HAPPENS. — WOODY ALLEN ⚡

2 MILES

N

★ PARKING

3RD CLASS

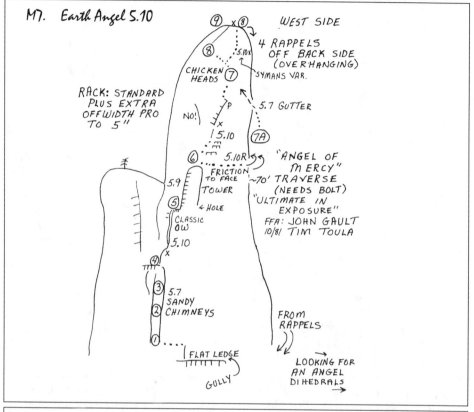

**M7. Earth Angel 5.10**

WEST SIDE

4 RAPPELS OFF BACK SIDE (OVERHANGING)

SYMANS VAR.

CHICKEN HEADS

5.10x

RACK: STANDARD PLUS EXTRA OFFWIDTH PRO TO 5"

5.7 GUTTER

NO! P

5.10

7A

5.10R

"ANGEL OF MERCY"

FRICTION TO FACE

~70' TRAVERSE (NEEDS BOLT)

"ULTIMATE IN EXPOSURE"

FFA: JOHN GAULT 10/81 TIM TOULA

5.9

TOWER

HOLE

CLASSIC OW

5.10

5.7 SANDY CHIMNEYS

FROM RAPPELS

FLAT LEDGE

GULLY

LOOKING FOR AN ANGEL DIHEDRALS →

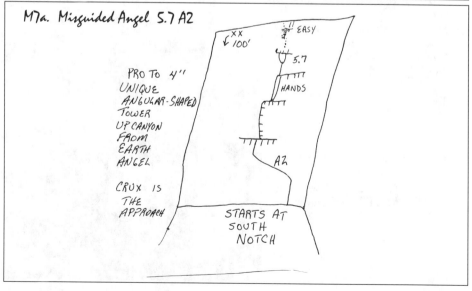

**M7a. Misguided Angel 5.7 A2**

XX 100'

EASY

5.7

PRO TO 4"
UNIQUE ANGULAR-SHAPED TOWER UP CANYON FROM EARTH ANGEL

HANDS

A2

CRUX IS THE APPROACH

STARTS AT SOUTH NOTCH

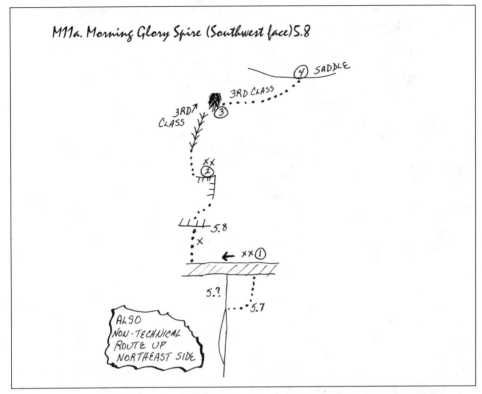

M11a. Morning Glory Spire (Southwest face) 5.8

8.  **Jap Head-Original Route 5.9** [G. Parker, Dan Bingham 1972 while pinned down by two of three people with rifles. Missed 'em by thiry feet.] Two pitches. Northwest corner.

9.  **N Face-Kamikaze Korner 5.9+R** [T. Coats, P. Davidson, D. Dawson 1980s.] Two pitches. North face crack/dihedral to broad face.

10. **Tower of Bootle 5.10** [P. Davidson, S. Grossman '80s.] One pitch. West of Japhead. Crack in notch on northeast side.

11. **Morning Glory Rock 4th Class** from northeast side.

11a. **Morning Glory Spire (Southwest face) 5.8** [M. Hill, D. Lindquist 1991.] Four pitches.

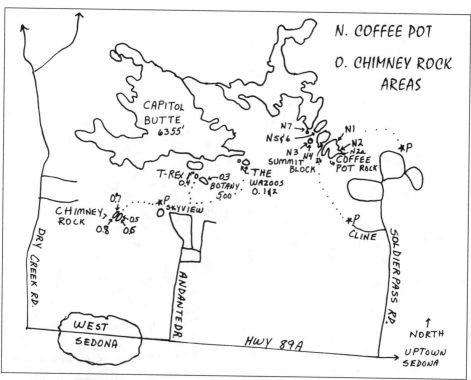

# N. COFFEE POT AREA

This list includes routes on formations in the immediate area of Coffee Pot Rock. Described east to west.

1. **Coffee Pot Rock-Original 5.9** [Dan Bingham, G. Parker 1972.] Eight pitches, mostly short. Pitch 1: 150' northeast "Indiana Jones" chimney. Pitch 2: Downclimb from notch to south face and southeast ledge traverse. Pitch 3: 5.7 crack system. Pitch 4: 5.9 diagonal seam to stance (optional belay) to bush and up to final 4th class ledge to east. Two 170' rappels off north. Neat mountaineering route. One of the top three summits in Sedona for views.

2. **Spout Route 5.11** [J. Mattson, T. Coats 1985.] Three pitches. Pitches 1 and 2: Rotten east face cracks. Pitch 3: To obvious off-width corner capped by roof.

2a. **South Spout 5.11** (5.10 C1) [M. Hill, D. Linquist, R. Thorne. FFA 1992.] Six pitches. Recommended.

2b. **Parker Route** [G. Parker] On tower immediately adjacent to Coffee Pot Rock. Southeast crack to rappels off west side.

3. **Summit Block Rock-Original Route 5.9 A2** [S. Baxter, R. Hardwick, K. Karlstrom, Whitfield, Erik Powell 1970s.] Two pitches. South face, 30' right of Dr. Rubo's Wild Ride.

N1. Coffee Pot Rock-
    Original 5.9

GEAR: STADARD RACK
    1 # 7 TRICAM
    1 # 5 CAMALOT
    2 # 4 FRIENDS

☑ ONE OF THE TOP
   3 SCENIC SUMMITS
   IN SEDONA

"CLASSIQUE"

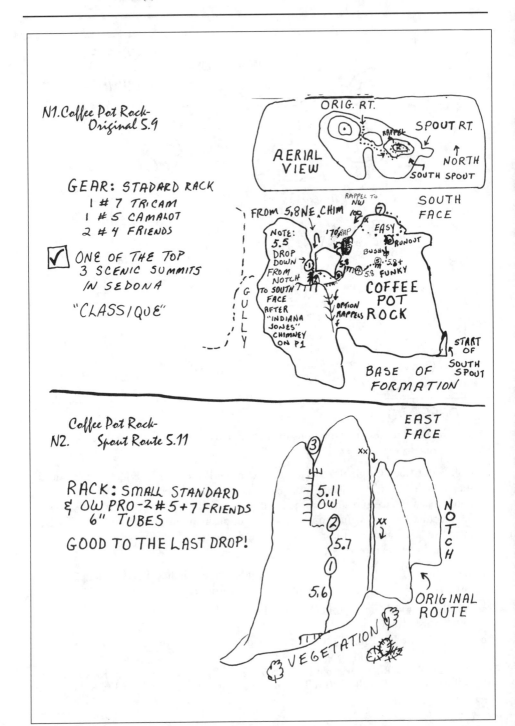

Coffee Pot Rock-
N2.     Spout Route 5.11

RACK: SMALL STANDARD
& OW PRO-2 #5+7 FRIENDS
    6" TUBES

GOOD TO THE LAST DROP!

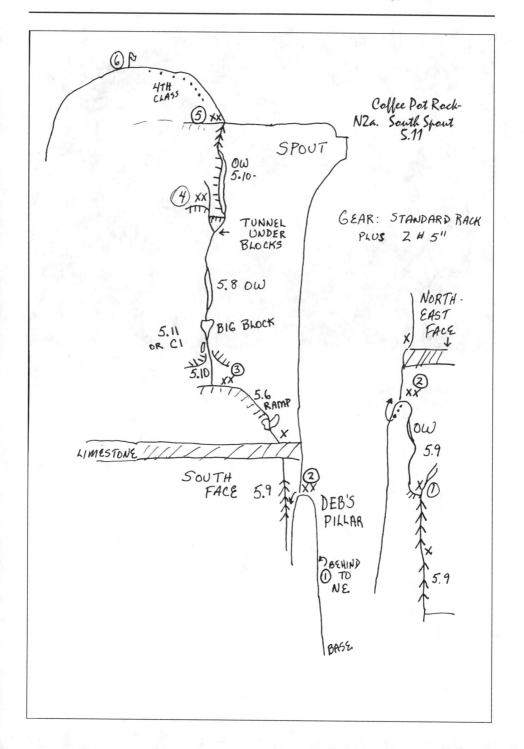

Coffee Pot Rock-
N2a. South Spout
5.11

GEAR: STANDARD RACK
PLUS 2 # 5"

Summit shadow and rappel anchor (juz kiddin') on Summit Block Rock

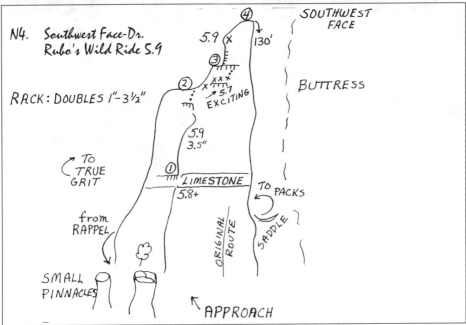

N4.  Southwest Face-Dr. Rubo's Wild Ride 5.9

RACK: DOUBLES 1"-3½"

SOUTHWEST FACE

5.9  X   130'

5.9 EXCITING

BUTTRESS

5.9 3.5"

TO TRUE GRIT

LIMESTONE 5.8+

TO PACKS

from RAPPEL

ORIGINAL ROUTE

SADDLE

SMALL PINNACLES

APPROACH

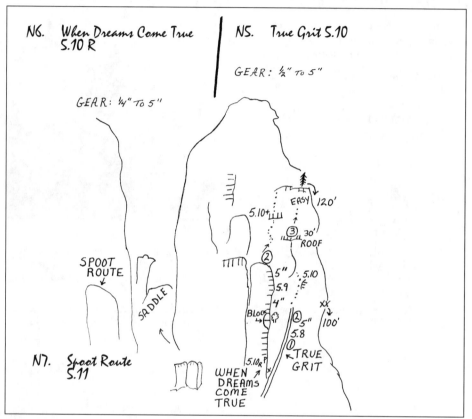

N6. *When Dreams Come True* 5.10 R

GEAR: 1/4" TO 5"

SPOOT ROUTE

N7. *Spoot Route* 5.11

N5. *True Grit* 5.10

GEAR: 1/2" TO 5"

EASY 120'

5.10+

3 30' ROOF

2

5" 5.10
5.9
4"
Block
2 5" 100'
5.8
1 TRUE GRIT

5.10R

SADDLE

WHEN DREAMS COME TRUE

4. **Southwest Face-Dr. Rubo's Wild Ride 5.9+** [L. and T. Coats, S. Baxter 1983 .] Four pitches. Classic cracks to airy face traverse to mantle. One rappel to east. Fun and popular.

5. **True Grit 5.10+** [S. Grossman, Dave Baker, Fig 1983.] Three pitches. Tower in notch (behind) north of Summit Block. Chimney to 30' roof.

6. **When Dreams Come True 5.10+R** [S. Grossman, Herb North, P. Davidson 1983.] Three pitches. Chimney to dihedral with tree. Goes left from Pitch 1 of True Grit after 15'.

7. **Spoot Route 5.11** [P. Davidson, J. Haisley, T. Coats 1980s.] One pitch. Fingercrack in north face of spire northwest of Original Route. Right of off-width crack. Reportedly good.

Area O

# O. CHIMNEY ROCK AREA

This area includes routes on spires directly east of Chimney Rock at the base of Capitol Butte to Chimney Rock itself. Described east to west.

Chimney Rock NE Face

1. **The Wazoos-Grand Wazoo 5.7** [G. Parker, D. Bingham, Al Marshall '70s.] Two pitch. South face.

2. **Little Middle Pecker Pinnacle** [G. Parker, D. Bingham '70s.] Two pitches. South face.

3. **Botany 500 5.8** [G. Parker, R. Hardwick 1970s.] One pitch. Northeast rotten crack system to pine tree rappel.

4. **T.Rex 5.10-** [J. Ingels, M. Peterson, RJ Gauer 1980s.] Two pitches. Spire. North to south face. Thrillin' finish,

5. **Chimney Rock-East (Lower) Tower-Red-Headed Stranger 5.9** [P. McFarlane, RJ Gauer, J. Ingels 1980s.] Two pitches. Southeast face. Pitch 1: Crack system to left-leaning ramp, limestone belay. Pitch 2: Up 20' to 15' right traverse to slot. One rappel to west. Exciting.

?6. **Little Red Heads Southeast Face 5.10X** [J. Symans, R. Ramirez, etal.] Three pitches. Starts left of Red-Headed Stranger at southeast corner. Pitch 1: Hand cracks to ledge.

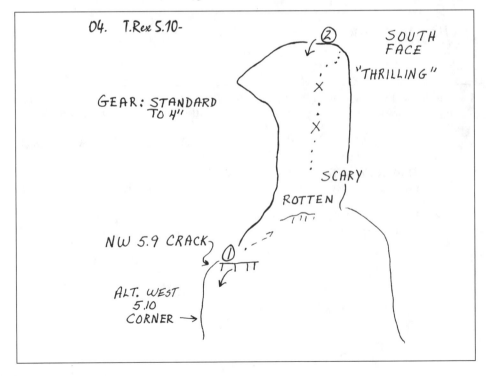

Pitch 2: Crack to classic right-slanting crack to crux 5.10X bulge (mantle, needs bolts) to knob runout.

7. **West Tower-North Face-Original Route 5.7** [B. Kamps etal 1950s.] One pitch. Chimney. An old squeeze.

8. **West Tower-Southwest Face 5.9** [K. Karlstrom, S. Baxter 1970s.] One pitch. Off-width.

Formations in areas O through N

# P. NORTHWEST AND WEST SEDONA

An extensive area of varying formations in the backcountry of the Secret Mountain Wilderness northwest of Sedona south to The Cockscomb (west of Chimney Rock). Described north to south.

1. **Secret Spire 5.9 A2** [R. Black, D. Houchin 1984.] One pitch. Beautiful needle (spire) obvious on right up Secret Canyon. Handcrack to aid.

2. **The Pagoda- Amen Ra 5.10** [P. Davidson, S. Grossman or S. Baxter, Al Doty 1980s.] Two pitches and 4th class. Tower/temple. Southeast face chimney to ledge system. Fourth class up east-northeast face to summits on butte. A long thrash up Boynton Canyon, see quads.

3. **Helicopter Spire-South Face 5.10-** [G. Rink, T. Toula 1992.] Three pitches. Hike 1 hr up Boynton Canyon to red rock spire on right.

4. **El Bandito Spire North Face 5.10-R/X** [T. and L.Coats 1980s.] One pitch. First 1st "hoodoo" spire just north of Boynton Canyon trailhead parking. Unprotected traverse to crack with stacked block.

5. **Aladdin's Lamp-West Face 5.11-** [S. Baxter, T. Toula, 1994.] One of Sedona's finer steep hand/fingercracks. Refer to map on page 45. Take Dry Creek Road to Road 5ZC North. Approach by hiking east on Soldier Pass Trail for 30 minutes. Small pinnacle on right is Aladdin's Lamp.

Area P

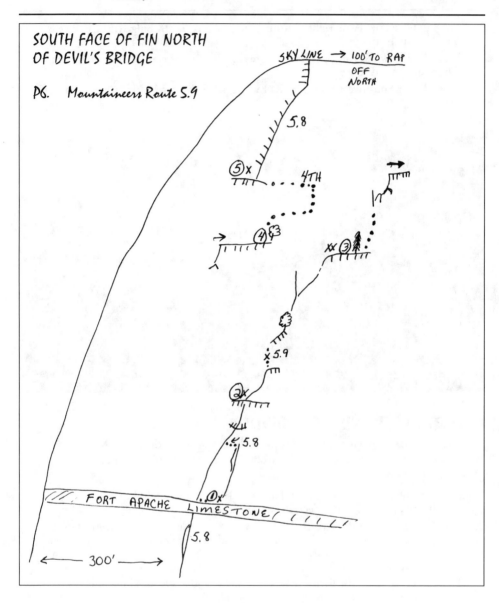

SOUTH FACE OF FIN NORTH
OF DEVIL'S BRIDGE

P6.    Mountaineers Route 5.9

SKY LINE → 100' TO RAP
OFF
NORTH

5.8

⑤x

4TH

④

XX③

X 5.9

②x

5.8

① x

FORT APACHE LIMESTONE

5.8

← 300' →

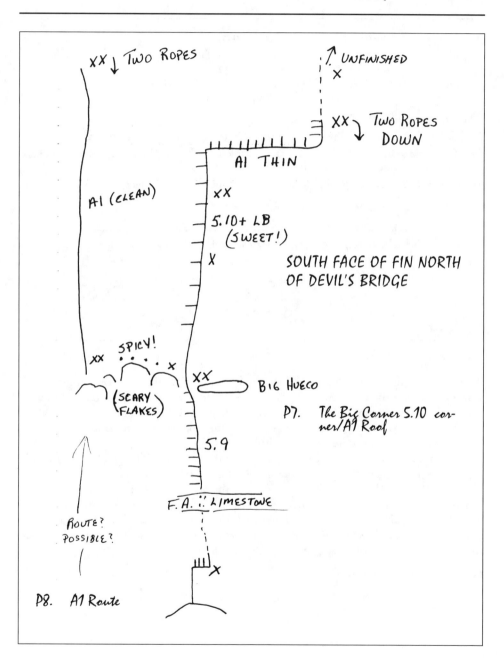

XX ↓ TWO ROPES

↑ UNFINISHED
X

XX ↓ TWO ROPES DOWN

A1 THIN

A1 (CLEAN)

XX

5.10+ LB (SWEET!)

X

SOUTH FACE OF FIN NORTH OF DEVIL'S BRIDGE

XX SPICY! ・・・・・ X

(SCARY FLAKES)

XX BIG HUECO

P7. The Big Corner 5.10 corner/A1 Roof

5.9

F.A. .". LIMESTONE

ROUTE? POSSIBLE?

P8. A1 Route

---

**South Face of Fin north of Devil's Bridge, Routes 6 through 8**

6. **Mountaineers Route 5.9** [M. Hill, Andrew and Glenda Lainis 2/91.] Six pitches.

7. **The Big Corner 5.10+ corner/A1 Roof** [M. Hill, T. Maloney 1993.] Three pitches. Directly north of Devil's Bridge. Excellent corner liebacking to A1 roof.

8. **A1 Route** [M. Hill, T. Maloney 1993.] One pitch. Clean aid.

**The Cockscomb Spires, West Sedona**

Middle two "golf tees." (Bring the #1 wood). Described from north to south.

9. **The China Brush 5.10-R** [T. Toula, G. Rink 1989.] One pitch. West face handcrack with "choss across" traverse. Simo-rappel.

10. **The Bullpen 5.7** [G. Rink, T. Toula 1989.] One pitch. West face, right-facing corner.

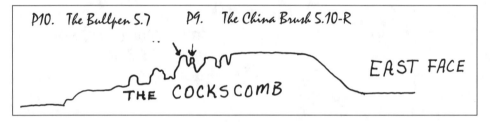

## THE STONE

A stone of fine size recently uncovered by the waters, was standing on a certain high place where a pleasant little wood ended at a rocky road, and it was surrounded by herbs and various flowers of all kinds of colors; and as it looked at the great numbers of stones all together in the road below it, the desire came to it to drop down there, and it said to itself, "What am I doing here with these little plants? I want to live with my sisters there." And down it dropped, and rolled to a stop among the comrades it longed for; and soon it began to be in constant travail from the wheels of the carts, the hooves of the iron-shod horses, and the traveller's feet: this one turned it, the other kicked it; sometimes a chip was taken off or, again, it was covered with mud or the dung of some animal; and it looked back in vain to the place it had departed from, to that place of solitary and tranquil peace. And this is what happens to those who desire to go from a solitary contemplative life to live in cities, among people of infinite evils.

Leonardo da Vinci Cod Atl fol; 175v-a

{The rest is silence.-Shakespeare-Hamlet Act V Sc 2}